The New Middle Ages

Series Editor
Bonnie Wheeler
English & Medieval Studies
Southern Methodist University
Dallas, Texas, USA

The New Middle Ages is a series dedicated to pluridisciplinary studies of medieval cultures, with particular emphasis on recuperating women's history and on feminist and gender analyses. This peer-reviewed series includes both scholarly monographs and essay collections.

More information about this series at
http://www.springer.com/series/14239

Christopher M. Roman

Queering Richard Rolle

Mystical Theology and the Hermit in Fourteenth-Century England

Christopher M. Roman
Kent State University
New Philadelphia, Ohio, USA

The New Middle Ages
ISBN 978-3-319-49774-7   ISBN 978-3-319-49775-4 (eBook)
DOI 10.1007/978-3-319-49775-4

Library of Congress Control Number: 2016959200

© The Editor(s) (if applicable) and The Author(s) 2017
This work is subject to copyright. All rights are solely and exclusively licensed by the Publisher, whether the whole or part of the material is concerned, specifically the rights of translation, reprinting, reuse of illustrations, recitation, broadcasting, reproduction on microfilms or in any other physical way, and transmission or information storage and retrieval, electronic adaptation, computer software, or by similar or dissimilar methodology now known or hereafter developed.
The use of general descriptive names, registered names, trademarks, service marks, etc. in this publication does not imply, even in the absence of a specific statement, that such names are exempt from the relevant protective laws and regulations and therefore free for general use.
The publisher, the authors and the editors are safe to assume that the advice and information in this book are believed to be true and accurate at the date of publication. Neither the publisher nor the authors or the editors give a warranty, express or implied, with respect to the material contained herein or for any errors or omissions that may have been made.

Cover illustration: Pattern adapted from an Indian cotton print produced in the 19th century

Printed on acid-free paper

This Palgrave Macmillan imprint is published by Springer Nature
The registered company is Springer International Publishing AG
The registered company address is: Gewerbestrasse 11, 6330 Cham, Switzerland

For Nicole,
And our boys, Jacob and Isaac
For me and my lufyng, lufe makes bath be ane

Acknowledgments

I would like to thank the faculty, staff, and students of Kent State University and the Tuscarawas Campus for their support in the work of this book. This book was begun while on a faculty professional improvement leave (FPIL) granted through the university, and the time given me helped immensely in getting this project off the ground, as well as in drafting two of the chapters. In particular, I would like to thank Beth Knapp for her unfailing faculty support, the student workers in the campus library for acquiring materials for me (to the point that they gave me my own shelf for requested books), as well as my faculty colleagues and good friends, Kathy David Patterson, Karen Powers, Ryan Hediger, Tony Dallacheisa, Adrian Jones, Jeremy Green, Jeff and Beth Osikiewicz, David Raybin, and Susannah Fein (especially for putting me on the path to be the medievalist I am today).

I am also thankful to my student assistants, David Embree for launching this project with work on an annotated bibliography on queer medieval studies, and Jonathan Miday, for his research, bibliographic compilation, and, most importantly, friendship.

Many of these ideas I tried out on my graduate seminar students who went along for the ride that was investigating the Medieval Mystical Text; I am thankful to Heidi Frame, Elizabeth (Betsy) Melick, Kimberly Beal, Hana Alghamadi, Maeed Almarhabi, Noah Grissett, and Devena Holmes.

I would also like to thank my friends in the large web that constitutes my big, queer, medieval studies family who have heard, read, or commented on previous versions of this work, or have provided support, friendship, and inspiration in a variety of ways too numerous to count and numinous to account for: Mike Ryan (*per la luce e la sagezza*),

Will Rogers, Michelle Sauer, Susannah Chewning, Angie Bennett, Dorothy Kim, Rick Gooden, Jeffrey Cohen, Eileen Joy, Myra Seaman, Jonathan Hsy, Dianne Berg, Robert Stanton, Stephanie Batkie (*for turning me on to acousmatics!*), Matthew Irvin, Damian Fleming, Rob Barrett, Dan Kline, Brantley Bryant, Paul Megna, Arthur Russell, Shyama Rajendran, Natalie Grinnell, Brian Gastle, Joseph Derosier, Heide Estes, Katharine Jager, Gabrielle MW Bychowski, Roberta Magnani, Asa Mittman, Bob Hasenfratz, Travis Neel, Andrew Albin, Kristi Castleberry, Diane Watt, Kara McShane, Karl Steel, Steven Rozenski, Lex Ames, Virginia Langum, Alaina Bupp, Josh Eyler, Andrew Pfrenger, Laurie Finke, David Hadbawnik, Anthony Bale, Jeff Stoyanoff, Julie Orlemanski, Cord Whitaker, Tim Jordan, Andrew Kraebel, Jamie Staples, Alan Montroso, Lara Farina, Denis Renevey, Karma Lochrie, Ann Martinez, Glenn Burger, Anne Harris, Mary Kate Hurley, Louise Nelstrop, and many, many others.

I want to thank Bonnie Wheeler at Palgrave MacMillan for supporting the project from its inception.

This book could not have been written without the support of my mother, Debora, and sister, Jaclyn, or that of my grandparents, Lois and Earl DiLulio, who, to this day, declare their pride and love for my work and what I have become: "from the little boy running around on the North Side to a professor." The deepest of thanks goes out to my longest and dearest friends, Lee McCracken and Patrick Donahue. Though we are scattered across the globe, our bonds of friendship remain strong, cemented with syrup and buckwheat cakes.

None of this would be possible without the unwavering love, support, laughter, and editorial acumen of my wife and life partner of nearly two decades, Nicole. As well, this book was both inspired by and distracted by (in a good way) the joy of other ways to be in the world—manifested in play, imagination, and comic books—represented by and in our children, the inimitable hooligans, Jacob and Isaac. Finally, our fur children, Groot and Buchi (1999–2016) provided the unbidden snuggles, cuddles, and lickish-love that only fur children provide.

Of course, all errors are my own.

Contents

1 Introduction: Queering the Hermit   1

2 Richard Rolle's Eremitic Ontology   25

3 The Phenomenology of the Open Body   55

4 Richard Rolle's Ecology of *Canor*: An Aesthetics of Desire   85

5 Epilogue: Three Vignettes   117

Bibliography   125

Index   139

CHAPTER 1

Introduction: Queering the Hermit

> *We must never settle for that minimal transport; we must dream and enact new and better pleasures, other ways of being in the world, and ultimately new worlds ... Queerness is essentially about the rejection of a here and now and an insistence on potentiality or concrete possibility for another world.*
>
> –José Esteban Muñoz

Abstract *Queering Richard Rolle* considers how Rolle navigates queer, eremitic conduct in order to create an identity always in process. I examine three aspects of Rolle's thinking throughout this work: his ontology, phenomenology, and sound ecology. These three aspects of his *oeuvre* invoke both a way of understanding being in the world, an opening up of the body in queer ways to experience the divine, and a way to consider divine contemplation in terms of singing the body.

Keywords Queer theology · Conduct · Hermit · Pride

The moment that Richard Rolle rejects his former life to become a hermit is a decidedly queer moment in its embrace of a new world. According to the *Officium* prepared by the nuns of Hampole for an ultimately failed canonization attempt, Rolle asks his sister to meet him in the woods with two pieces of her clothing. Upon receiving these clothes, he cuts the sleeves from the grey tunic, attaches them to the white tunic, and "effigiaret confusam similtudenim heremite" [fashions himself hermit robes].[1]

His sister thinks he has gone mad, shouting "frater meus insanit, frater meus insanit" [my brother is crázy, my brother is crazy][2] and runs off. Her reaction to Rolle's coming out as a hermit is noteworthy in that his transformation echoes the modern discourse of the closet,[3] but she rejects him in his coming out, shocked at both the destruction of her garments and the incomprehensibility of his new identity—the forest setting, the revealing of identity, the forging of a new path are liberatory for Rolle. "Insanit" becomes a shorthand for non-normative, for queer. She may as well have exclaimed, "*You're one of those?*"[4] His literal self-fashioning as a hermit begins a queer journey in which Rolle defines himself in opposition to normative structures of family, wealth, church, and theology.[5]

Richard Rolle considers not only how the hermit interacts and critiques the world around him but also how the hermit is queer in its relation to world. As Tison Pugh suggests, "the Western medieval world lacked a hermeneutic sense of homosexuality *contra* heterosexuality as a defining feature of an individual's identity, yet this predominantly Christian culture faced continuous struggles in defining the proper role of love and eroticism for its people."[6] Rolle's expressions of love and eroticism often place him in hostile environments—he moved around from place to place seeking eremitic stability. His anti-systematic thinking and theology speaks to the very queer struggle of the hermit in medieval life. As Rolle presents us with the destabilization of identities, he invites a refiguring of the body, senses, and being in the presence of divine events. Systematization in Rolle's work is antithetical to the local manifestations of queerness exhibited by the contemplative, the hermit, and the mystical.

Queering Richard Rolle utilizes a queer and post-structural framework to think about Rolle's sense of ontology, phenomenology, and ecology. I use the critical term "queer" for thinking about Richard Rolle's work because of the non-normative and disruptive potential of his eremitic life. Despite its ahistoricism, concepts of the queer are germane to Rolle's project as he attempts to bring worlds into being, articulates an eroticism and desire rooted in aural-being, and puts forth a disruptive praxis that resists easy definitions of the eremitic life. As Annemarie Jagose points out, "queer describes those gestures or analytical models which dramatise incoherencies in the allegedly stable relations between chromosomal sex, gender, and desire."[7] The queer hermit is in constant dialogue with the Christian thought around him, but offers up critique, in the orientation of an incoherent desire that cannot be contained in linguistic or rhetorical frameworks involving God, as well as the creation of life that challenges the very stability of the world itself. In this way, queer "operates as a third term, beyond the gender/sexuality opposition" allowing me to consider the hermit as "not strongly marked as a category of selfhood, nor [...] institutionalized as such."[8] By eschewing clear boundaries of self and institution, the hermit lives a life of queer process, always making a life, disrupting normative paths of love, rather than conforming to any one Christian identity. As Glenn Burger and Steven F. Kruger point out, "a certain stabilized idea of medieval sexuality is crucial to the schemes of historical suppression that see modernity emerging from an 'other' world."[9] Rolle's cross-dressing, peripatetic, eremitic life challenges the very stability of a definitive religious identity and asks that readers reconsider religious life and thinking in the Middle and modern ages as he forges new paths of devotion. In borrowing from past Christian practices and imagining new forms of religious living, Rolle works with José Esteban Muñoz's project to "never settle for that minimal transport; we must dream and enact new and better pleasures, other ways of being in the world, and ultimately new worlds."[10]

What we have of Rolle, besides his biographical moments, is copious writing—epistles, treatises, lyrics, sermons, exegesis. In thinking with Rolle in *Queering Richard Rolle*, I want to open a dialogue between post-structuralist and queer theory and theology and medieval eremitic and mystical theology. My transhistorical, queer work offers a way to consider not only religious identity formation in the Middle Ages, but also to think about how the medieval is "dissonant and resonant" in contemporary thought, "how modernity is not formed out of the past, but how present and past are in constant dialogue insuring that neither one can claim a sure-footed ground in time."[11] As Rolle represents his relationship with the divine, neither divine space and time, nor material space and time, remain within set definitions.

As a way into Rolle's particular queer eremiticism, I want to first situate Rolle's work within a Foucauldian framework regarding counter-conduct, asceticism, and mysticism. As well, queer theology works with Foucault to situate the disruptive potential of theology. As Marcella Althaus-Reid writes of her queer theology, "let us consider that without rupture there is no salvation, for restoration, like salvation obeys the theological compromises of a different order, the field of engagements, not of new beginnings."[12] Michel Foucault identifies the mystical in the Middle Ages as a site for counter-conduct toward a Church hierarchy whose law overlooks and may even suppress the individual's experience of God. In other words, with

Althaus-Reid, we can imagine that the hermit struggles in a "field of engagements," a kind of religious *life* that is a site of disruption for the medieval church. The rise in the numbers of hermits in the mid-Middle Ages paralleled an increase in the writing of various manuals, which attempted to define the solitary religious life. Such manuals as Grimlaicus' *Rule for Solitaries* or the oft-translated *The Myrour of Recluses* created a code of conduct that attempt to circumscribe the life of the solitary. These manuals suggest that the eremitic life, one that valued a form of living that claimed authenticity against that of contemporary religious living, was as problematic for the Church as mysticism itself.[13]

The hermit poses a challenge to a medieval Church that emphasizes rule, order, and discipline since oversight of their life could be virtually non-existent. The case of Richard Rolle is important, as he took on the mantle of hermit himself, and he never received any kind of church endorsement. As well, he forged his life out of a struggle with concepts of medieval sin, such as Pride and Lust, which placed him in a queer position in terms of relationships with his surrounding community. Despite his lax attitude toward asceticism, his representation of eremiticism was highly influential in his local community and through manuscript dissemination, beyond. His eremitic life and example inspired religious movements toward affective spirituality in the Late Middle Ages.[14] Rolle challenges a monolithic medieval Christianity in that he practiced a form of living at a local level, placing him in dangerous positions. The Church structures could absorb such practices, edit them, or suppress them.[15]

For Rolle, the hermit expresses a specific kind of project of individual religious life that reshapes desire for the divine, placing them in the queer waters of theology; desire for God places the hermit in a world of sensory reconfiguration that challenges the very terms of what it meant to be a human and a hermit. A queer theologian "is a theologian in/of exiles."[16] Exile is an important aspect of Rolle's theology as it places him in a liminal position that allows him to configure erotic desire for God in non-normative ways. Although terminology surrounding the eremitic and anchoritic life could overlap, as I will discuss, the hermit led a religious life rooted in the lives of the Desert Fathers and Mothers of early Christianity. Hermits could move around. Hermits may stay in place. Hermits could be connected to monasteries. Hermits could go rogue. Hermits could be near-saints. Hermits could be criminals. Eremiticism is a way of life that challenged institutional forms of religious living instilled by the

Church by reaching into the past and reimagining the wilderness. A queer wilderness in various shapes and guises becomes a counterpoint to normative Christian practices.

As well, the hermit exists in the struggle between two strains of Christian life that Michel Foucault identifies as *exomologesis* and *exoagouresis*. On the one hand Rolle strove to continually verbalize his thinking, what Nikolas Rose calls rendering "oneself truthfully into discourse,"[17] and, yet, because of the role of the hermit-as-exile, he also worked to undo that self. As Foucault writes, "we have to sacrifice the self in order to discover the truth about ourselves, and we have to discover the truth about ourselves in order to sacrifice ourselves."[18] Rolle uses the life of the Church as inspiration, but his manner of living and the content of his writings posed a critique of the Christian community, rituals, and institutions, as well as proposing alternate ways to experience the divine and work in the world. As Althaus-Reid comments, "we can know God better through a radical negation of the way of closeted knowing found in the tradition of the church and theology. This is the Queer, stranger God who in our time and age is showing Gods face amongst people who are God's lovers—and Queer lovers at that."[19]

Before delving into eremiticism in the Middle Ages, it is worth considering the kinds of religious lives available to the medieval Christian devotee. The monk or nun, for example, lived an institutionally sanctioned life within the rules set out by the order and the Church. Even the Franciscans, who initially challenged the practices of the Church through street preaching and a commitment to poverty, were eventually absorbed into the monastic forms of the Church and the order devolved into internal strife that led to charges of abuse and materialism.[20] The anchorite and hermit constitute other forms of religious life that followed the contours of monastic living, while often setting themselves apart, rejecting the values of the surrounding world. Anchorites lived a religious life confined to an anchorhold that was connected to a church or other sanctioned space. Women were more often anchorites than men and there is much critical discussion of the inherent sexism to anchoritic practices as a way to corral female religious life as well as anchoritic practice as a source of agency for women in a Church filled with misogynistic thinking.[21] Hermits lived a looser religious life, and, perhaps, this is why the eremitic life is more difficult to categorize. It may have posed a category problem since the life of the hermit did not necessarily conform to any *particular* rule, often cobbling together a rule as they lived or claiming to live a rule outside the confines of a monastery or cell.

The hermit exhibited a kind of "erotohistoriography" in terms of their self-fashioning. As Elizabeth Freeman writes, "erotohistoriography is distinct from the desire for a fully present past, a restoration of bygone times. Erotohistoriography does not write the lost object into the present so much as encounter it already in the present, by treating the present itself as hybrid. And it uses the body as tool to effect, figure, or perform that encounter."[22] The eremitic life was an attempt to express a Christian life of a previous time, reaching into past practices as a way to live in the contemporary age with the "encounter" of God.

Eremitic values often conflicted with social norms, as well. Rolle's eremitic living poses a great refusal in its nomadic way:

> [T]he nomadic Queer is the image of the unstable or irredeemable body of a theological subject who loves amidst insecurity and risk. The question in theology is about how Queer lives do theology: they wander into each other's spaces, digress at points of desire, position and reposition themselves amongst themselves and amongst others, and, eventually participate in creation of new (partial) conceptualizations of love and God.[23]

The hermit's very lifestyle rejected traditional concepts of community, wealth, or family that stood as pillars of Western pastoral power. At the same time that the hermit was marked by their rejection of structures of normality, they were also celebrated as important members of the community. The hermit could fulfill a societal niche such as gatekeeper or forest-developer. The hermit lived a life that transformed societal strictures, and, by performing that very life, they also posed a serious critique of the very nature of Christian-being. As John McSweeney writes, religious transgression has "the capacity to disrupt a thought."[24] While posing this destabilization, however, they also were admired, respected even, for choosing to live a life that was deemed authentic and following the contours of a Christianity unavailable to the parish. The hermit was a material reminder of another kind of Christian life.

In his March 1, 1978 lecture, Michel Foucault defines conduct as "the activity of conducting (*conduire*) [...] but it is equally the way in which one conducts oneself (*se conduit*), lets oneself be conducted (*se laisse conduire*), is conducted (*est conduit*) and, finally, in which one behaves (*se comporter*) as an effect of a form of conduct (*une conduite*) as the action of conducting or of conduction (*conduction*)."[25] This definition opens up a key issue in thinking about the hermit. Hermits conduct *themselves* in many aspects of day-to-day life. This kind of nomadic, self-conduct adds a nuance to Foucault's definition of conduct since his definition indicates both that the conducted submits to those who conduct, and also, that the form of conduct is an effect of conduction. Yet, hermits themselves use models of conduct that do not require oversight and sometimes oversight is unavailable in terms of their movements from community to community or physical remoteness from a community. As Rotha Mary Clay writes in her seminal work on hermits and anchorites in medieval England: "the solitary was canonically appointed and placed under definite rule, but every age has its free-lances. The difficulty connected with due order and discipline were as old as the sixth century monachism."[26] Clay categorizes hermits and anchorites throughout her analysis utilizing their setting as a marker of the life they led. For example, there are hermits who are cave-dwellers or fen-dwellers, while others lived in the gates of cities. Clay's analysis follows a biological taxonomy popular in the late-nineteenth and early-twentieth century, but as is evident within her efforts toward taxonomy, the life of the hermit poses significant categorical challenges.

The queering of the hermit, then, can be viewed through this matrix: eremitic living is revered, but "no one oversees their activities."[27] As Foucault writes of pastoral power, "to accept the authority of another means that each of the actions that one will be able to perform will have to be known or, in any case, will have to be able to be known by the pastor, who has authority over the individual and over several individuals [...]."[28] Yet, pastoral power may have little effect on those who are not routinely overseen such as the hermit. Thus, there was suspicion cast over their behaviors. As Clay writes, "the hermit should make obedience to God alone, because he himself is abbot, prior, and prefect in the cloister of his heart."[29] Anchorites, for example, were enclosed and usually assigned a priest who was their confessor and sometime amanuensis. The hermit, although licensed to preach, did not have their activity so fully under observation. As the medieval poet, William Langland, critiques eremitic life in his medieval poem, *Piers Plowman*, "like a hermit without an order he forms a sect by himself with no rule and no law of obedience."[30] From Langland's brief aside, we may speculate that forging a Christian life outside of well-defined boundaries, such as a monastery or nunnery, was met with suspicion, criticism, and doubt in some circles.

The lack of well-defined boundaries is evident in other documents pertaining to hermits, as well. In the *Benediction of a Hermit* from the sixteenth century, the only indication of what a hermit is to do in his chosen vocation comes from this passage said by the Bishop after the "converses" has donned his newly blessed vestments:

> Brother, behold we have bestowed upon you the dress of a hermit and, together with it, we admonish you to live in purity, sobriety and holiness. Pass your time in vigils, in fasting, in work and prayer, and in the works of mercy so that you may possess eternal life and so live forever and ever. Amen.[31]

The vagaries of this passage are repeated in other benedictions of hermits such as the one found in MS Lambeth 192 fol. 46 and the so-called *Benediction of St. Celestine* in Sloane 1584, and indicate that within each of these benedictions a hermit may choose to fulfill eremitic expectations in a variety of ways.[32] After the benediction is over it is recommended that the bishop should educate the hermit more in "hermitic" ways. Those ways are not clearly defined. This instruction is mostly taken up with the prayers he should say at various times of the day, but it also dictates that the hermit should not be idle and should spend time doing civic works (such as road building) or making his own food.

This loose rule of hermits made them targets for more conservative strains of religious thinking, as well. In 1389, for example, Richard II passed an anti-vagrancy statute to deal with men who had taken on the life of a hermit without proper identification from their ordinaries.[33] Foucault's work in religious studies assists in thinking about the eremitic life and the challenge it posed in its queerness. To return to his March 1, 1978 lecture, Foucault highlights asceticism and mysticism as two aspects of counter-conduct in medieval Christianity. For Foucault, "asceticism is [...] a sort of tactical element."[34] Mysticism, escapes pastoral power in that it is the "privileged status of an experience" as the "soul sees itself."[35] These two tactics find their way into Rolle's form of eremitic being as they are key to his queer eremiticism. With the exile inherent in eremitic identity—whether physical or mental—the hermit is attempting to create a fluid space to see the soul outside of the abilities of pastoral power to create.

Foucault is highlighting the possibility of a queer mode of Christianity. One, as Mark Larrimore writes, that is "a scandal to law, foolishness to thought. Its appetite for disruption is prophetic."[36] With this kind of scandalous practice, Foucault points out in a much earlier essay that mysticism was "incapable of dividing the continuous forms of desire, of rapture, of penetration, of ecstasy, of that overpouring which leaves us spent: all of these experiences seemed to lead, without interruption of limit, right to the heart of divine love of which they were both the outpouring and the source returning upon itself."[37] The normative requests that these are kept separate, the queer refuses. This mystical tradition running parallel to the eremitic life reveals the transgressive capability of combining the two projects of asceticism and mysticism. By creating a life that is always already crossing boundaries, pastoral power is unable to fully account for the eremitic or mystical. This combination of projects perhaps finds its best realization in a struggle to define a rule for hermits and thinking about how hermits create a form of living.

RICHARD ROLLE, HERMIT

We can see the controversy over the eremitic life in a new light when we consider the difference between rules and a *form of living*. Giorgio Agamben writes, "the form is not a norm imposed on life, but a living that in following the life of Christ gives itself and makes itself a form."[38] Boundaries, in the form of rules or manuals, become a field of transgressive play in queer theology. This form of play in queer theology experiments with the reterritorializing of God: "reterritorialisation is [...] precisely that act of making new connections or re-codings of reality once an original context has been superseded."[39] As I will discuss throughout *Queering Richard Rolle*, Rolle is attempting to live a life in a form that disrupts traditional notions of following Christian law (the Ten Commandments, the Church hierarchy) and resists easy categorization while delineating further the power of counter-conduct to institutional forms of power.

Richard Rolle's path to the eremitic life could best be described as unusual. The contours of Richard Rolle's life are as follows.[40] Rolle was born in Thornton Dale c. 1295 and died c. 1349 in Hampole, both in Yorkshire, possibly from the Black Death. He went to school briefly in Oxford, but left the university in pursuit of what he considered a more authentic Christian life. His *Officium* and *Miraculum*, prepared by the nuns of Hampole who attempted to seek Rolle's canonization, declares that his leave from Oxford was a desire to avoid "maximus hiis qui uacant carnis lasciuiis" [those who give themselves to fleshly lusts].[41] He was never officially sanctioned to be a hermit. His identity concretized through performance. He requested that his sister bring him two tunics, one grey and one white. He took these vestments from her, and then he cut the garments in order to make an approximation of a hermit's uniform. Upon seeing Rolle cut up her clothes, his sister thought he had gone mad and ran away. As Virginia Davis remarks, the vestments of a hermit were key to their identity. They signified "humility of heart, chastity, and contempt for world and worldly things."[42] From this point on, Rolle wandered. As Frances Comper phrases it, "although a wanderer he was a hermit, and although a hermit a wanderer."[43] Rolle's change of habitation often resulted from discord with the families he chose to advise. He was accused of criticizing his female benefactor's fashion choices too harshly, inappropriate touching of women, as well as general over-zealousness in his eremitic role. Rolle chides himself for these actions. Rolle ended his days as confessor to the nuns of Hampole, writing various texts for one Margaret Kirkby, a nun and then anchorite living on the grounds. It is believed that Margaret Kirkby furthered his "cult" when she moved to a cell close to Rolle's burial site and had a hand in the writing of the *Officium* and *Miraculum*.

According to Nicholas Watson, Rolle's defensiveness in his works stems from the fact that "his life as a hermit was still sufficiently unusual to cause suspicion, give opponents room for criticism, and put him on the defensive."[44] Watson also continues to point out that it is difficult to even call Rolle unusual because of the wide variety of hermits: from Carthusians to the author of *The Cloud of Unknowing*, to Walter Hilton before entering an Augustinian canonry.[45] In Watson's estimation, Rolle's works created an authoritative eremitic identity for himself as well as exhibiting a lack of systematic theology that reveals him to be, in a word, "idiosyncratic."[46] While holding up Rolle's forging of authority, it is difficult to ignore the, perhaps, denigration of Rolle in Watson's use of the term "idiosyncratic."[47] In fact, *Queering Richard Rolle* celebrates the idiosyncrasy of Rolle and his thought. Rolle's concern with his lived experience situates him queerly in relation to medieval forms of normative living. This queerness trickles down, as well, to his writing, which often uses his own struggles to forge a fluid identity under the auspices of eremiticism. Despite the variety of eremitic vocations, it may be fruitful to think of Rolle's concept of eremitic identity as continually forged from adversity. The hermit existed in queer spaces and ways of thinking that challenged the very notion of a stable Christian identity. In this way, the very generic concerns regarding vernacular theology are challenged in Rolle's work.[48]

For the rest of this introduction, I want to entertain the concept of pride as a common theme that runs throughout Rolle's work and some of the eremitic writing that he influenced. This theme challenges normative concepts of sin in order to offer up pride as a site of adversity for Rolle's creation of a life. In not rejecting sin and instead utilizing it as a site of struggle and identity formation, this discussion serves as a rubric for thinking about Rolle's ontology, phenomenology, and acousmatic, divine ecology in the remainder of this book.

Eremitic Pride

Pride becomes a catalyst for Rolle's eremitic identity since it is so important to struggle with it, tame it, and reorient it under a different intentionality. There is a challenging thread in Rolle's work: what if we became hermits? In other words, the self-fashioning that Rolle employs often undermines stable religious identities by challenging concepts of inner intent and devotion to a nomadic life. Before looking at Rolle's work with pride, it would be fruitful to explore sin as an evolving concept as a way to think about how Rolle is adapting and transforming pride to shape a particular form of eremitic identity.

Augustine defined pride or *superbia* as a sin where the sinner desires to be as God. For Augustine sin is inherited through the disobedience of Adam and Eve, thus original sin is passed down to Christians through sexual intercourse. As Patrick Cheng points out, original sin is linked to actual sin (sins like lust, gluttony, and pride) as sins turn Christians onto themselves or "incurvatus in se." This selfishness, then, separates Christians from God and neighbor. However, as Cheng points out, Augustine's definition of sin must be seen in the context of his argument with Pelagius who argued that Christians could save themselves through following God's will. Augustine disagreed with Pelagius (and ultimately won the argument) because Pelagian ideas robbed God of his sovereignty. Thus, original sin is a condition, while committing sins are acts.[49]

From Gregory the Great to Aquinas, however, sin has been taxonomized in various ways. In the Bible itself sins are organized under issues of rebellion, disobedience, transgression, wickedness, or debt.[50] The sin of pride could be the gateway to other sins or the culminating seduction after overcoming all the other sins. Commentators point to the examples of Lucifer and Adam as representatives of pride. Siegfried Wenzel suggests that for many patristic writers, pride either was the gateway to the other sins or occurred "when one has *overcome* any or all of the six other vices."[51] The Oxford University Press recently published a paperback series on the Seven Deadly Sins. These books were originally lectures born from collaboration between the New York Public Library and the Oxford University Press. The minister and writer, Michael Eric Dyson, suggests real, positive benefits to pride, especially in the black (and, I may add, queer) community. His formulation of Aristotelian pride, "owning up to one's true moral achievement and expecting others to follow suit is by no means an act of vanity or conceit. The virtue of pride, or as Aristotle terms it, 'proper pride' is the means found between extremes of empty vanity and undue humility."[52] Dyson later points out, "If Aristotle's 'proper pride' is a virtue to blacks whose self-respect has been battered, then white pride is often the vice that makes pride necessary."[53] Pride is integral in battling both homophobic and racist sentiments woven into the discourse of subjection that marks hetero- and white normativity. Thus, utilizing sin becomes a way to overcome the pressure to deny the self. Queering pride becomes a reaction to a wider hegemonic injustice—it is an important identity constructed out of relationships within conflict and adversity. Aristotle himself points out that pride is "a sort of crown of the virtues for it makes them greater, and it is not found without them."[54] Thinking with the unstable definitions of pride available to us historically, Aristotle's formulation is worth bearing in mind since Rolle's own commentary on pride seems on the surface, counter-intuitive as pride becomes a site for self-mortification *and* self-creation. Rolle excoriates the people who relish in pride as a form of denying themselves, but relishes pride for its availability to shape the eremitic life as a just life. As Foucault writes, "mortification is a kind of relation from oneself to oneself. It is a part, a constitutive part of the Christian self-identity."[55] Rolle attempts to articulate an ethics of pride: it is the "fracture between being and praxis."[56] In understanding Rolle in Aristotelian terms, a *proper* pride, we can understand Rolle's high valuation of the contemplative life while critiquing the normative activity of lay and religious leadership.[57]

To situate Rolle in terms of the revolutionary mysticism that Foucault outlines in his lectures reveals the limits in the relation between pastoral power and mystical revolution. Pastoral power may indicate the normalization of the Christian soul in terms of defining sinful behaviors and prohibitions, while eschewing the individual's experientially-based spirituality. Mystical revolution, then, shows how sinful behavior may be transformed in the self-fashioning of the individual Christian to something positive while rejecting normalizing hierarchies and identities.

Rolle's semi-autobiographical work, the early *Incendium Amoris* (dated by Watson as written before 1343) utilizes pride as a way to queer eremitic practice. Pride is either bound with normative Christian practice or it is intertwined with humility to define the struggles of the hermit. In this early work, Rolle is working with pride as it affects his own struggles. The *Epistle of St. Machari*, which Ralph Hanna calls "integral to (and perhaps inspired by) the particular self-fashioning by which [Rolle] created himself as hermit and spiritual guru"[58] puts pride at the forefront of the discussion on eremitic life.

In order to provide a genealogy of eremitic identity as born of pride, I am beginning with the later *Epistle of Saint Machari* (dated to the 1380s). This will provide a finishing point to the use of pride so that we may see how Rolle influenced such works. In the *Epistle* the hermit begins with discussing self-knowledge. As the hermit begins to know himself, he will see all of his faults. This will result in confession and penance.[59] As Rose points out, "in confessing one also constitutes oneself."[60] However, this confession and penance can lead to troubles for the hermit: "þus þou has synned, bot þou has done þi pennaunce, ande þi synnes [er] forgyffen þe. Now art thy haly."[61] Pride comes from a space where the hermit has struggled with identity, sin, confession, and yet, despite this process, new sin appears. The *Epistle* goes on to indicate that when this sense of pride develops, the other sins quickly follow. In his attempts to combat pride, the hermit may feel that it is hopeless. As God has taken away his support to show the hermit that he needs God, God slowly gives back strength to the hermit saying: "takes my ȝok vpone ȝoue and [l]ers of me, for I am mylde and meke in hert."[62] What is remarkable about this sense of pride is the inevitability of it; the affliction of pride indicates that the hermit is on the right path. He has taken stock of his past life and made amends for it. But, this has cleared the way for sins that he wanted to avoid in the first place. The establishment of a holy life does not prevent the hermit from the same pitfalls; and, as is clear in this *Epistle*, the holy life may set up the hermit for further and more difficult tribulations. Despite the return to sin, the hermit will realize more than ever his greater connection to God and the hermit's need for *kenosis*. To fall, to fail, to struggle, is to find oneself emptied and closer to the holy life than if one had followed a straight path. The hermit must use sin as a confirmation of the worth of the eremitic life.

This eremitic struggle with pride is even more pronounced in the *Incendium* where Rolle defines hermits as those who

> live loving God and their neighbor; they despise worldly approval; they flee, so far as they may, from the face of man; they hold all men more worthy than themselves; they give their minds continually to devotion; they hate idleness; they withstand manfully the pleasures of the flesh; they taste and seek ardently heavenly things; they leave earthly things on one side without coveting them; and they find their delight in the sweetness of prayer.[63]

Eremitic identity cannot be formed without community rejection. In the *Incendium* it is the contemplative and the contemplative life that Rolle defines that is the highest and most worthy. The worth comes out of the separation of eremitic identity from the "regular" Christians. The *intent* of the hermit must be clear to live the holiest of lives.

Intentionality and Exomologesis

The ethic of intention revolves around the "examination of external acts versus internal motive."[64] Intentionality parallels what Foucault identifies as *exomologesis:* "a way for the sinner to express his will to get free of the world, to get rid of his own body, to destroy his own flesh and get access to a new spiritual life. It is the theatrical representation of the sinner as willing his own death as a sinner. It is the dramatic manifestation of the renunciation to oneself."[65] Intention is a problem that Richard Rolle returns to in many of his works, for he is very condemnatory of those who appear holy, but are not. It is Rolle's method of defining the normative to his queer. Rolle repeats this difficult matrix in much of his work; people's outward holiness serves as a cover for their own sinfulness. As well, his own eremitic actions indicate his own holiness; his often unorthodox movements reinforce his inner intentions to the holy life. Disruption and a rejection of orthodox practice reify the power of the holy life. Intentionality is important in understanding Rolle's concept of pride because there are often condemnations of the same actions he himself is performing as a hermit. The difference, then, is in the intent of those actions. Thus, sin can mean different things and cause different outcomes. In a word, Rolle queers sin itself releases its multivalent, positive effects.

Richard Rolle's concern with pride in *Incendium* ranges from problems regarding hypocrisy in people who outwardly seem holy but are not to concerns over his own actions and the (wanted) condemnation he garners for his actions. Rolle's emphasis on self-knowledge as born of Pride finds expression in Foucault's own analysis of the Cynic's self-knowledge in which "the Cynic changes the value of this currency and reveals that the true life can only be an other life in relation to the traditional life of men, including philosophers."[66] Rolle would add theologians, as well. Rolle attempts to utilize theological concerns to make the hermit a recognizable subject. Early in *Incendium*, Rolle writes that there is no room for loving God and loving things of the world. His example for this is those who are "reprobates," who "admittedly go to church and even pack it to the doors: they beat their breasts and heave great signs, but none of this means a thing. Seen of men they may be; heard of God they are not."[67] This outward show where they outwardly appear to be God-fearing only to be internally thinking of their possessions or the possessions they want to have is Rolle's standard definition of a lack of life-formation. But, these are "everyday" parishioners.

Queer critiques resist normative absorption. Queer narratives disrupt straight teleological narratives. Rolle holds condemnation for certain kinds of contemplatives who seek bureaucratic positions and leave the eremitic life behind. Rolle writes: "those contemplatives who are most on fire with the love of eternity are like those higher beings whose eagerness for eternal love is most enjoyable and outstanding. They never, or scarcely ever, engage in outside activity, or accept the dignity of ecclesiastical preferment or rank."[68] Here Rolle begins to fine tune his definition of the role that a contemplative plays in the world. For him, a true contemplative never sullies himself with ecclesiastical roles. These roles are not worthy of the contemplative, and although he uses a humility *topos* to assure the dignity of station, in this same section he indicates that God has a place for each Christian; refusing position is an act of humility that carries much ethical weight. As Judith Butler points out, "ethical deliberation is bound up with the operation of critique."[69] Only by being outside is Rolle able to critique traditional notions of pride and define the eremitic life apart from the traditionally churched. When Rolle turns to hermits, those who eschew public positions shine the brightest: "if anyone wants to polish them, as it were, by loading them up with honors, he will only diminish their ardour [...]. And if they themselves accept public office and dignity, they do in fact demote themselves and become less worthy."[70] Even the holiest of people, who have accepted their place, still "rejoice in the thought that after death their name may be honoured by those who follow them."[71] Rolle's emphasis here is in not reaching stability; the *struggle* is the hallmark of hermit-being.

Other actions also contribute to a hermit succumbing to the wrong pride. Thus far, Rolle is using pride to mark those with false intentionality. Seeking knowledge and engaging in talk lead to problems, as well. Rolle writes, "it is love that delights the soul and sweetens the conscience, because it draws it away from lesser pleasures and from the pursuit of one's own glory. Knowledge without love does not edify or contribute to our eternal salvation; it merely puffs up to our own dreadful loss."[72] Rolle condemns theologians who search out knowledge: "an old woman can be more expert in the love of God—and less worldly too—than your theologian with his useless studying. He does it for vanity, to get a reputation, to obtain stipends and official positions. Such a fellow ought to be entitled not 'Doctor' but 'Fool'."[73] In the same vein, Rolle condemns the heretic with his "undisciplined and chaotic mind, blinded by its desire for its own reputation [...]."[74] The contemplative seeking a place in the bureaucracy of the Church, the theologian after self-indulgent knowledge, the heretic after his reputation are all wanting to go higher: "if you want to know what God is, you are wanting to be as God—and that is all wrong. Face the fact: only God can know himself."[75] God is the model of self-knowledge, one the hermit must learn themselves.

There is another aspect of pride that Rolle wrestles with and that is the feeling of pride that may result from insults. This struggle is directly applicable to Rolle's forging of eremitic identity through adversity. As McSweeney points out regarding Foucault's engagement with religion: "the paradoxical Christian self thus constitutes an 'other' of his thought, which he allows to affect it, drawing it beyond its limits."[76] Rolle's version of pride marks the turn to the personal, and thus, a reflection of a technology of the self, drawing the hermit beyond the limits of sinful prohibitions. Rolle writes, "it would seem to be undoubted that an insult is better than honour, confusion than success, grief than glory. It is by these latter things that a man often lapses into vainglory. Yet if he habitually faced the former with patience he would learn humility in this life here [...]."[77] The recipe of honor, success, and glory will lead to pride; the other terms, insults, confusion, grief leads to a cultivation of humility. Yet, what is marked about *Incendium Amoris* is how much of the right kind of pride is found in humility. Rolle relishes receiving insults and grief.

Rolle uses sin as a rupture in his losing of self in order to present or discover himself in hermit-being.

Rolle often, indirectly, defends an action of his by indicating (usually in the third person) that he has undergone a criticism, but then turns around to defend that action. He does not bear his own advice here and take the insults, instead choosing to forge his eremitic identity from these. In this way he is articulating the "me" from the "not-me" within each pride-event. Rolle is able to utilize the discourse of spirituality for its "politics of continual transformation by holding up what we can be and what is not yet seen."[78] For example, Rolle writes on the subject of the contemplative's joy:

> [T]here are those who disapprove of laughter and others who praise it [...] surely that which springs from a cheerful conscience and spiritual buoyancy is worth praising? [...] Yet when we are cheerful and joyful the irreligious call us dissolute and when we are serious they call us hypocrites! It is unusual for a man to assess as good in another what he does not find in himself [...]. It is the act of a presumptuous man to think that is others do not follow his own particular way of life they are depraved and deceived! And the cause of it all? He has let go humility.[79]

The normative Christian cannot see the queer in Rolle's hermit. The conflict with pride is evident; to forge an eremitic identity Rolle has had to undergo a certain level of scrutiny and insults. His defense of his life choice has resulted in further entanglements with pride.

Exile, penance, and purgation are important elements in eremitic identity. As Tom License indicates, "a hermit's personal exile was viewed as a sort of earthly purgation. The idea that penance and purgation were two names for a continuum by which the soul was restored to perfection, the first being usually the name of the process of life, the second its name after death, went back to St. Augustine."[80] Exile is intimated in the rejection bound to the insult. Rolle exhorts those who choose to pursue the religious life: "people rejoice in honors and are delighted by applause—and this I find true of some who have a reputation for sanctity of life. Such people seem to me either too holy for words, or else complete fools, though men call them wise and learned."[81] Therefore, knowing the self will result in knowing if one is truly right before God. Rolle's method for knowing if one is truly a contemplative is his own rubric involving becoming "self-narrating beings."[82] Rolle writes, "but if in his self-investigation he finds he is glowing with the heat and sweetness of divine love beyond description, and he is setting out on the contemplative life and is committed thereto" then one might be a contemplative.[83] Here Rolle points to self-knowledge, knowing if one is truly a contemplative. That identity is wrapped in Rolle's own method, his own experience. The conflict of pursuing the contemplative life and the act of knowing if one is truly a hermit are intertwined in Rolle's thought.

These iterations of pride prove productive in their attempt to render eremitic identity; the hermit is not striving, the hermit is singular, the hermit bears insults, but knows that this is a proper life. The hermit possesses self-awareness that saves him from traditional concepts of pride, as *superbia*, to use the sin as a salvific gesture. As Judith Butler writes, "if the question of power and the demand to tell the truth about oneself are linked, then the need to give an account of oneself necessitates the turn to power, so that we might say that the ethical demand gives rise to the political account, and that ethics undermines its own credibility when it does not become critique."[84] The *Incendium* forges its queer, eremitic ethics from the framework of the critique of intentionality. Pride is to be pushed aside *and* held dear; the intention of embracing pride is not to denigrate the self, but to defend a kind of life. Pride and identity in this case are intertwined, even though the Augustinian definition of Pride as being like God, is not the pride, in fact, that Rolle wrestles with at all.

Becoming-hermit is a continuing process. Aristotle's sliding scale of pride more accurately informs Rolle's methodology: the falsely humble hermit who accepts a higher bureaucratic position; on the other end, the churchgoer whose ritual sparks a sense of pride in their behavior. The hermit is proud in his chosen path only because it is a virtuous person, born of the conflicts around them, who bears that pride. For Rolle, only this proper pride befits the hermit. As Foucault formulates it, the pride of the hermit is akin to "the relation to the truth [as] established in the form of a face-to-face relationship with God and in a human confidence with corresponds to the effusion of divine love" that is indicative of the mystical and ascetic traditions.[85] In his forging of eremitic life, and in the demands of the face-to-face encounters, Rolle is remapping a Christian body in terms of Foucault's positive *parrhesia*.

Queering Richard Rolle considers how Rolle navigates this queer, eremitic conduct in order to create an identity always in process. I examine three aspects of Rolle's thinking throughout this work: his ontology, phenomenology, and sound ecology. These three aspects of his *oeuvre* invoke both a way of understanding being in the world, an opening up of the body in queer ways to experience the divine, as well as a way to consider divine contemplation in terms of singing the body.

In Chapter 2, I expound further on the relationship between eremitic being and the place of the hermit in the community by investigating Rolle's ontological concerns in his theology. The experience of God on earth is contingent on placing the hermit outside traditional structures. This requires the hermit to redefine space and time, as well as renegotiate the relationship between the hermit and the community. As is clear in Rolle's work, the hermit is defined out of the community, but this does not mean that the hermit leaves the neighbor behind. The very ontological nature of love is integral in eremitic being, and, thus, Rolle spends much time in considering the being of love itself as a way to orient the hermit in the world, as well as, in time.

Chapter 3 considers Rolle's phenomenology in terms of his mystical experience. In narrating his experiences, Rolle wrestles with the problem of language as testament to the mystical experience of opening the body to its queer possibilities. By placing the body beyond normative sense structures, the body opens to the queer indwelling of the divine connecting the soul to a queer temporality of now and future simultaneously. Rolle filters the senses through the experience of fire, sweetness, and song that refuse sensual and theological systematization.

In the final chapter, I return to Rolle's concept of *canor* and consider a divine sound ecology that works through Rolle's work. Rather than emphasize God's love visually as many mystics do, Rolle experiments with the ineffability of sound, an acousmatics, in order to express an ecological relationship, one in which the singer inhabits the sound of God and, thus, renders the body porous as sound permeates it. Rolle's use of the lyric reveals the enmeshed quality of singer, song, divinity, and body. In this way, Rolle's lyrics create environments that queer the "field of relations." The gift of *canor* in Rolle's work creates a performative aspect to contemplative living. Rolle's experiment with sound and lyric opens up a divine ecology that intermediates between singer and God.

This book reads queer theory and theology back into the Middle Ages and the life of the hermit, Richard Rolle. In the Epilogue, I read Rolle's queerness forward into contemporary literature, politics, and music to underscore queer eremiticism and the various forms it takes, bubbling back to the surface, touching lives in surprising ways, suggesting new forms of being. Rolle's work refuses closure by imagining and reimagining the divine touch found in *fervor, dulcor,* and *canor.*

Notes

1. *The Officium and Miracula of Richard Rolle, of Hampole*, ed. Reginald Maxwell Woolley (New York: Macmillan, 1919), p. 24.
2. *Officium*, p. 24.
3. See Eve Kosowsky Sedgwick, *Epistemology of the Closet* (Berkeley: University of California Press, 1990).
4. This phrase is borrowed from Sedgwick's discussion of Racine's *Esther*, p. 78.
5. As Robert Mills points out in his analysis of this incident compared with a miniature of Jerome in a dress in the *Belles Heures of Jean de Berry*, "figurative identification with aspects of the feminine could be valued positively in male religious environments in a way that actual displays of androgyny and cross-dressing were not," p. 7. *Seeing Sodomy in the Middle Ages* (Chicago: University of Chicago Press, 2015).
6. Tison Pugh, *Chaucer's (Anti-)Eroticisms and the Queer Middle Ages* (Columbus: Ohio State University Press, 2014), p. 5.
7. Annemarie Jagose, *Queer Theory: An Introduction* (New York: New York University Press, 1997), p. 3.
8. Robert Mills, *Seeing Sodomy*, p. 21.
9. Glenn Burger and Steven F. Kruger, "Introduction," *Queering the Middle Ages*, ed. Glenn Burger and Steven F. Kruger (Minneapolis: University of Minnesota Press, 2001), p. xiii.
10. José Esteban Muñoz, *Cruising Utopia* (New York: New York University Press, 2009), p. 1.
11. Steven F. Kruger, "Medieval/Postmodern: HIV/AIDS and the Temporality of Crisis," *Queering the Middle Ages*, ed. Glenn Burger and Steven F. Kruger (Minneapolis: University of Minnesota Press, 2001), p. 278.
12. Marcella Althaus-Reid, *The Queer God* (London: Routledge: 2003), p. 40.
13. For a discussion of various anchoritic and eremitic texts and the homoerotic anxiety within see Michelle M. Sauer, "Uncovering Difference: Encoded Homoerotic Anxiety witin the Christian Eremitic Tradition in Medieval England." *Journal of the History of Sexuality* 19.1 (2010): 133–152.
14. For a discussion of Rolle's influence in Yorkshire after his death especially as related to his patrons and Margaret Kirkby's influence see Jonathan Hughes, *Pastors and Visionaries: Religion and Secular Life in Late Medieval Yorkshire* (Woodbridge: Boydell, 1988), especially pp. 84–88.
15. Barry Windeatt argues that the *De Excellentia Contemplationis*, a late-medieval compilation of Rolle's work, is an attempt to "edit and re-read Rolle into more acceptable forms" (211). See "1412–1534: texts" in *The Cambridge Companion to Medieval English Mysticism*. Eds. Samuel Fanous and Vincent

Gillepsie (Cambridge: Cambridge University Press, 2011). See also A.I. Doyle, "Carthusian Particpation in the Movement of Works of Richard Rolle Between England and Other Parts of Europe in the 14th and 15th Centuries." *Kartäusermystik und—mystiker, Analecta Carthusiana* 55.2 (1981): 109–20.
16. Althaus-Reid, *The Queer God*, p. 20.
17. Nikolas Rose, *Governing the Soul: The Shaping of the Private Self*, 2nd. edn. (London: Free Association, 1999), p. 222.
18. Michel Foucault, "About the Beginning of the Hermeneutics of the Self," *Religion and Culture: Michel Foucault*, ed. Jeremy Carette (New York: Routledge, 1999), p. 179.
19. Althaus-Reid, *The Queer God*, p. 171.
20. For what he calls the "painful institutionalization" of the Franciscan movement see André Vauchez, *Francis of Assisi: the Life and Afterlife of a Medieval Saint*. Trans. Michael F. Cusato (New Haven: Yale University Press, 2012), especially pp. 94–103.
21. See Nancy Warren's *Anchorites and Their Patrons in Medieval England* (Berkley: University of California Press, 1985). Julia Hassel. *Choosing Not to Marry: Women and Autonomy in the Katherine Group* (New York: Routledge, 2002). *Religion and Sexism: Images of Women in the Jewish and Christian Traditions*, ed. Rosemary Radford Reuther (Eugene, OR: Wipf and Stock, 1988).
22. Elizabeth Freeman, *Time Binds: Queer Temporalities, Queer Histories*. (Durham: Duke University Press, 2010), p. 95.
23. Althaus-Reid, *The Queer God*, p. 50.
24. John P. McSweeney, "Religion in the Web of Immanence: Foucault and Thinking Otherwise After the Death of God." *Foucault Studies* 15 (Feb 2013): p. 77.
25. Michel Foucault, *Security, Territory, Population: Lectures at the College de France 1977–78*, ed. Michel Senellart. Trans. Graham Burchell (New York: Palgrave, 2004), p. 195.
26. Rotha Mary Clay, *The Hermits and Anchorites of England* (London: Methuen, 1914), p. 89.
27. Henrietta Leyser, *Hermits and New Monasticism: A Study of Religious Communities in Western Europe: 1000–1150* (New York: Macmillan, 1984), p. 78.
28. Michel Foucault, "Sexuality and Power (1978)," *Religion and Culture*, ed. Jeremy R. Carrette (New York: Routledge, 1999), p. 124.
29. Clay, p. 88.
30. Quoted in Virginia Davis, "The Rule of Saint Paul the First Hermit." *Monks, Hermits, and the Ascetic Tradition*, ed. W. J. Sheils. (Padstow: T.J. Press, 1985), p. 205.

31. *Hermitary: Resources and Reflections on Hermits and Solitude.* http://www.hermitary.com/articles/benediction.html (March 2016).
32. *M.S. Lambeth 191* and *Sloane 1584.* Unpublished translations. Ed. and trans. Michelle Sauer.
33. Davis, p. 206.
34. Foucault, *Security Territory, Population,* p. 207.
35. Foucault, *Security, Territory, Population,* p. 212.
36. Mark Larrimore, "Introduction," *Queer Christianities: Lived Religion in Transgressive Forms.* Eds. Kathleen T. Talvacchia, Michael F. Pettinger, and Mark Larrimore (New York: New York University Press, 2015), p. 4.
37. Michel Foucault, "A Preface to Transgression (1963)." *Religion and Culture,* ed. Jeremy R. Carrette (New York: Routledge, 1999), p. 57.
38. Giorgio Agamben, *The Highest Poverty: Monastic Rules and Form-of-Life.* Trans. Adam Kotsko. (Stanford: Stanford University Press, 2013), p. 105.
39. Althaus-Reid, *The Queer God,* p. 60.
40. For a fuller exploration of biography see Hope Emily Allen's "Introduction" to *English Writings of Richard Rolle: Hermit of Hampole* (Oxford: Oxford UP, 1963) and Frances M.M. Comper's *The Life of Richard Rolle* (New York: Barnes and Noble, 1928).
41. *The Officium and Miracula of Richard Rolle of Hampole,* ed. Reginald Maxwell (London: MacMillan, 1919), p. 23. Translation based on Frances M. M. Comper, *The Life of Richard Rolle* (New York: Barnes and Noble, 1928), p. 301.
42. Davis, p. 209.
43. Comper, p. ix.
44. Nicholas Watson, *Richard Rolle and the Invention of Authority* (Cambridge: Cambridge University Press, 1991), p. 43.
45. Watson, pp. 43–44.
46. Watson, p. 54.
47. In fairness, Watson comes to appreciate Rolle's thinking by the end of his book, *Richard Rolle and the Invention of Authority.* See especially pp. 268–69.
48. For a discussion of queering genres themselves see Tison Pugh's *Queering Medieval Genres* (New York: Palgrave MacMillan, 2004). Early on Pugh remarks, "the authorial process of queering genres depends upon the shock of narrative, its ability to jolt audiences into positions unanticipated, unexpected, and perhaps undesired," p. 3. Rolle's work is often jolting, challenging many traditional religious identities, which may have led to his perceived persecution from various circles.
49. Patrick S. Cheng, *From Sin to Amazing Grace: Discovering the Queer Christ.* (New York: Seabury, 2012), p. 19.
50. See Mark E. Biddle, *Missing the Mark: Sin and Its Consequences in Biblical Theology* (Nashville: Abingdon, 2005).

51. Siegfried Wenzel, "The Seven Deadly Sins: Some Problems of Research." *Speculum* 43 (1968): p. 4.
52. Dyson, Michael Eric. *Pride.* (Oxford: Oxford University Press, 2006), p. 16.
53. Dyson, p. 45.
54. *The Basic Writings of Aristotle*, ed. Richard McKeon. (New York: Random House, 1941): p. 992.
55. Michel Foucault, "Pastoral Power and Political Reason," *Religion and Culture: Michel Foucault*, ed. Jeremy R. Carette (New York: Routledge, 1999), p. 143.
56. Giorgio Agamben, *The Kingdom and the Glory: For a Theological Genealogy of Economy and Government.* Trans. Lorenzo Chiesa (Stanford: Stanford University Press, 2011), p. 54.
57. As Virginia Burrus notes, "for asceticism and queerness are, arguably, heavily overlapped terms: both designate practices that center on *resistance* to normative discourses of sex and sexuality," p. 147. "Queer Father: Gregory of Nyssa and the Subversion of Identity." *Queer Theology: Rethinking the Western Body*, ed. Gerard Loughlin (Malden, MA: Blackwell, 2007).
58. *Richard Rolle: Uncollected Prose and Verse* (Oxford: Oxford University Press, 2007), p. xiii.
59. *Richard Rolle: Uncollected Prose and Verse*, p. 93.
60. Rose, *Governing the Soul*, p. 244.
61. *Richard Rolle: Uncollected Prose and Verse*, p. 94.
62. *Richard Rolle: Uncollected Prose and Verse*, p. 95.
63. Richard Rolle, *The Fire of Love*, ed. and trans. Clifton Wolters. (London: Penguin, 1972), p. 83.
64. Elizabeth Zimmerman, "'It is not the deed but the intention of the doer': The Ethic of Intention and Consent in the First Two Letters of Heloise." *Modern Language Studies* 42.3 (2006): 249.
65. Michel Foucault, "About the Beginning of the Hermeneutics of the Self," *Religion and Culture: Michel Foucault*, ed. Jeremy Carette (New York: Routledge, 1999), p. 173.
66. Michel Foucault, "28 March 1984: First Hour." *The Courage of Truth: The Government of Self and Others II, Lectures at the College de France 1983–1984*, ed. Frédéric Gross. Trans. Graham Burchell. (New York: Palgrave MacMillian, 2011), p. 314.
67. Richard Rolle, *The Fire of Love*, p. 50.
68. Richard Rolle, *The Fire of Love*, p. 53.
69. Judith Butler, *Giving an Account of Oneself* (New York: Fordham University Press, 2005), p. 8.
70. Richard Rolle, *The Fire of Love*, p. 91.
71. Richard Rolle, *The Fire of Love*, p. 91.

72. Richard Rolle, *The Fire of Love*, p. 58.
73. Richard Rolle, *The Fire of Love*, p. 61.
74. Richard Rolle, *The Fire of Love*, p. 61.
75. Richard Rolle, *The Fire of Love*, pp. 62–63.
76. John McSweeney, "Religion in the Web of Immanence," p. 93.
77. Richard Rolle, *The Fire of Love*, p. 69.
78. Jeremy Carette, "Rupture and Transformation: Foucault's Concept of Spirituality Reconsidered." *Foucault Studies* 15 (2013): p. 71.
79. Richard Rolle, *The Fire of Love*, p. 72.
80. Tom License, *Hermits and Recluses in English Society: 950-1200*. (Oxford: Oxford University Press, 2011), p. 120.
81. Richard Rolle, *The Fire of Love*, p. 73.
82. Butler, p. 11.
83. Richard Rolle, *The Fire of Love*, p. 73.
84. Butler, p. 124.
85. Michel Foucault, "28 March 1984: Second Hour" *The Courage of Truth: The Government of Self and Others II, Lectures at the College de France 1983–1984*, ed. Frédéric Gross. Trans. Graham Burchell. (New York: Palgrave MacMillian, 2011), p. 337.

CHAPTER 2

Richard Rolle's Eremitic Ontology

> [...] because ontos is always a question of ethos and praxis. In that sense, the tone of a thing tells us more than anything else what it is, for its tone is its ethic, its practice, its ontology, its rapport.
> —fragilekeys;http://fragilekeys.com/2012/04/26/common-ontology/

Abstract Rolle explores the relationship between eremitic being and the place of the hermit in the community by investigating the ontology of the divine. To experience God on earth it is contingent to place the hermit outside traditional structures. This requires the hermit to redefine space and time, as well as renegotiate the relationship between the hermit and the community. As is clear in Rolle's work, the hermit is defined *contra* the community, but this does not mean that the hermit leaves the neighbor behind. The very ontological nature of love is integral in eremitic being, and, thus, Rolle spends much time in considering the being of love itself as a way to orient the hermit in the world, as well as, in time.

Keywords Ontology · Love · Being · Queer space · Queer temporality

Richard Rolle's ontology recognizes this "rapport" between *ethos* and *practice* in the uncovering of deception that leads the hermit to misunderstand the world, and the eventual *revelation* of the work of God already in the world through queer, disruptive eremitic practices. This eremitic ontology demands the recognition of the hermit's difference, their queerness, from a normative world in order to see the potential of their colocality with the divine. Queerness configures the eremitic self as severed from the self. For Lee Edelman the open-endedness of queerness "deliberately sever[s] us from ourselves, from the assurance, that is of *knowing* ourselves." Thus, there is the promise of the "better" that "does not assure happiness [...]," rather "it names only the insistent particularity of the subject, impossible fully to articulate and 'tending toward the real'."[1] Rolle is concerned with recognizing the particularity of the hermit in opposition to normative constructions of a Christian identity. As Linn Marie Tonstad writes, "the self is freed to be shaped and reshaped across time because at every moment of time it stands in relation to God as the source of its possibilities."[2] The queer project Rolle embarks upon is in knowing the self in its tendencies toward God. Rolle's eremitic ontology involves not only constructing the hermit's being from a positive outcome of sin but also discovering the field of relations and colocality that the hermit shares with the divine. God becomes more legible, though resistant to closure, in Its queer touch as It orients itself as love in Rolle's process of hermit-being.

The eremitic life must wrestle with the unknown of God—by attempting reclamation of ways of being, the hermit touches the past, while living with the "truth" of mysticism, the experience of a formless, unknowable, queer God that touches the world in unexpected ways. To think of God beyond grand normative narratives leads Rolle to question received religious ontologies as a way to stage the self-creation of identity, in this case, eremitic identity. Reading Richard Rolle with a queer and speculative realism lens renders God an object that has surfaces and withdraws and is connected with certain assemblages that make his contemplation possible to begin with. In other words, the recognition of a being of God is possible in terms of a queer eremitic ontology, which reveals God in terms of Its excessive, queerness in world.

I am beginning with ontology, specifically an eremitic ontology, because before moving on to Rolle's phenomenology and ecology in the next chapters, I want to present Richard Rolle's ontological concerns. In order to propose a phenomenology in his *oeuvre*, Rolle first attends to the hermit's concern, or, to put it another way, the hermit's *being*. The invisibility of different ways of beings is a critical focus of queer theology. As Marcella Althaus-Reid comments, "learning to see as a methodological step, is in itself a sexual challenge for Christianity. Theology, though influential systems [...] maintains the sexual metaphors of heterosexuality in their conditions of invisibility and pervasiveness. This invisibility is what stops us from questioning."[3] Eremitic being is most legible when it questions normative religious life so as to bend the body, space, and time to make multiple and multivalent modes of religious experience possible. As Kevin Hart writes "the Christian experience of God is that he has left his trace in the life and death of Jesus, that consequently it both is and is not an experience. One could say, loosely, that Christianity involves an experience of absolute interruption."[4] As well, Elizabeth Stuart argues, "queer theory itself nudges the theologian towards a different horizon [. . .] toward the eschatological and mysterious, to the sacramental heart of the Christian tradition."[5] Rolle's concern in his work is a queer concern, showing how, ontologically speaking, the recognition of the world and its patina of deception is necessary for the process of hermit-*being* in order for that hermit to experience and join in with the absolute interruption that is intertwined with Love.

How does one recognize an invisible God to love in the world? This chapter focuses on Rolle's contemplative manual, *The Form of Living*. In this text, Richard Rolle explores the ontology of Love in what could be visualized as a chart of Being with two axes. On one axis, Rolle explores the being of the contemplative *in* love as an eremitic *ethos*. On the other axis, Rolle sets out the being of Love itself as *praxis*. The question of how to love God is found on this second axis. Rolle points the hermit toward the God-object in order to be touched by the burning fire, *fervor*. In order for *fervor* to be experienced, Rolle emphasizes stability: "verray love is to love hym with al þi myght stalworthy, in al þi hert wisely, in al þi soule deuotely and sweetly."[6] A stout might, a wise heart, a devout and sweet soul—these three elements constitute the gift of the contemplative to God. The contemplative offers up their "might" by which Rolle means will, heart, and soul. The hermit uses these three potentials—a generating Trinity within—to return the touch of the elusive and queer, withdrawing God-object.

In investigating Rolle's notion of both the practice and being of the hermit and the being of God-Love, it is worth examining closely how he discusses the very notion of what-is and how the "what-is" is queer in terms of the normative being surrounding the hermit. As Graham Ward writes, "an orientation toward ontology—some model of the relationship between existence and existents, being and becoming—is necessary. The question also presupposes that an enquiry into the relationship is possible. The question demands that there is or can be an identification of a 'thing,' an understanding of thinghood."[7] For Ward, the debate surrounding the ontological nature of God is between God as beyond and God in the Augustinian sense, as source. For Ward, then, the debate is between a philosophical and theological line of questioning one in which the former is contained in the latter (for Augustine, and, thus, Ward). Ward's concern with "thinghood" is important for the sense of the God-object that I want to explore in Rolle's ontology. For Ward "its 'thinghood' and the varieties of 'thinghood' of which it is composed that are never stable, never static. Its thinghood is in suspension, as the 'what' is what it is in the fullness of its becoming."[8] Ward further elucidates, "whether a thing is can never be fully defined. That there *is* can be affirmed, but the nature of that *is* is not a thing that can be grasped or even experienced as an *is*, as presence, as that which can be isolated as present to itself."[9] Ward writes that it is only in the line of questioning do we have a sense of God's presence, but we will never know God-in-himself; "the questioning of God (both subjective and objective genitive) never ends; it just plumbs deeper into the mystery of the Godhead as the Godhead unfolds its own infinite nature."[10] We return to the event of interruption; it is in this interruptive *aporia* that the divine touch presents itself in infinity.

Rolle wants to open the hermit to love fully, to make the hermit vulnerable to Love's ability to unsettle the subject in the world. Slavoj Žižek comments, "in true love, 'I hate the beloved out of love'; I 'hate' the dimension of his inscription into the socio-symbolic structure on behalf of my very love for him as a unique person."[11] For Žižek, inscription places *limits* on love, reducing love, and in Rolle's case, misleads the hermit into loving the wrong kinds of things. It is in Rolle's eremitic ontology that this "socio-symbolic" realm is punctured and Žižek's "absolute" can be seen. Žižek writes that the Absolute is "something that appears to us in fleeting experiences—say, through the gentle smile of a beautiful woman, or even through the warm, caring smile of a person who may otherwise seem ugly and rude: in such miraculous but extremely *fragile* moments, another dimension transpires through our reality."[12] Žižek points to these fragile moments as queer (though he does not use this word), non-normative experiences requiring a recognition from the margins of time. Rolle's eremitic ontology insists that the experience of the hermit is rendered legible in these fragile moments in the margins. It is in Žižek's discussion of "uncoupling"—"as every Christian knows, love is the *work* of love—the hard and arduous work of repeated 'uncouplings' in which, again and again, we have to disengage ourselves from the inertia that constrains us to identify with the particular order we were born into"[13] that we see the hermit's challenge: to continually uncouple from normativity and not fall into categorical rigidity that leaves the hermit unsatisfied and destroyed, as well as avoiding the rigidity of fundamentalism in that the smile from the ugly goes unrecognized because the "ugly smile" has not met the hermit's own predetermined sense of where a smile should derive. Rolle's queer theology assists in continually keeping open the possibility of the divine and the resistance to these preconceived modes and categories of being.[14] This chapter attempts to give shape to Rolle's ontological concern as he examines deception, space, time, and the hermit's body as a way to describe a queer, eremitic sensuality, one that perceives the divine in disruption, meditation, and love.

RECOGNIZING DECEPTION IN *THE FORM OF LIVING*

Rolle's contemplative manual, *The Form of Living*, written at the end of his life for the nun Margaret Kirkby, focuses on recognizing deception.[15] Deception needs to be punctured in order to recognize the Real, in this case, a divine Real. On the surface, Rolle's text focuses on how to live the solitary life, however, Rolle spends a majority of the time defining the problem of reality. On the one hand, there are many things that lead the solitary astray: the devil, the flesh, sin. On the other hand, there is a reality beneath these obstacles—a way to live beside them that reveals the excess of divine being. Sin is central and normative while the divine takes up the queer spaces that refuse to be incorporated into sin. Much like the discussion of the struggle within the event of pride in Chapter 1, the normative structures of the world are necessary for recognizing the queer Real in which the hermit-being is formed. Sin is understood not as a crime-based model, rather Rolle (and queer theologians) rethinks sin in terms of a separation from a becoming-self and God.[16] This is not to say that Rolle is arguing that sin is not real; as he repeats, it is sin that will lead the soul to everlasting torment that is without comparison. However, that reality—the reality of sin—is at the same time a deception—it leads one to live falsely and deny the self by separating one from God so that the solitary does not know who they are, does not *allow* themselves to be touched by God. It is also necessary to recognize deception, to struggle through deception, because passing out of the stage of sin produces the furniture of the hermit's room.

If the fundamental question of ontology is "what is?" then *The Form of Living* investigates that question through the lens of the contemplative's connection to God. Therefore, Rolle is concerned with separating how what *is* relates to that which *negates*. For Rolle, the problem of ontology is finding the ways in which the solitary can fulfill their capability. Grace Jantzen's insights on a queer theology assist me in thinking through Rolle's attempt to "uncouple" the hermit from traditional frames of reference. Jantzen is interested in a theology that "gets rid of the straight and narrow boundaries of traditional Christendom and is open to difference, fluidity, curvature."[17] This fluidity and curvature finds fulfillment in the aesthetics of the self:

> those of us who already take up queer positions have some extra practice in the creativity and the cost of an aesthetics of the self. We are learning how to dig deep into our best possibilities, and not to allow ourselves to become flat mirrors of our contexts, reflecting and reinforcing its self-perceptions […] the mirror we hold up to our culture, religious and secular, is a mirror of curves and corners that reveals the multiple distortions of discursive and material reality.[18]

Rolle repeats in many of his works the formula "knowest thi self."[19] The need to know oneself is integral in understanding the life of solitude, as well as how that life opens toward God.[20] Rolle's eremitic ontology is based on defining what the hermit is, how to arrange eremitic space, and how the process of eremitic being opens up into a life devoted to God.

At the heart of Rolle's ontology is the role of God in the eremitic life. Ironically for a life that is predicated on solitude, the role of the hermit is saturated in relationships, relationships that I define as queer in terms of their intimacy and vulnerability with an Other whose very response to the touch of the hermit resists clear categorization. God is revealed through the connections between solitary and God. In other words, God is the something over there, something undefinable. The solitary's relationship with the *unknown* is where they find God. So, God resists the focus of the camera; God is not a stable object, but instead, something definable in terms of movement, in terms of the ability to love. God is a moving target that one can only miss. God is negated when the relationship between God and solitary is disrupted by sin-as-separator, deception, or falsity. Early in *The Form of Living*, Rolle warns that people are not what they seem. It is easy to see "worldisshe men and wommen that vsen glotony or lecherie and other oppyn synnes, bot þei ben also in sum men þat semen in penaunce and in good lif."[21] Rolle emphasizes the word "semen" and "seemeth" throughout his manual. Worldly people wallow in gluttony and lechery, so it is easy to see what to avoid in their case; they are actively and publicly sinning. However, Rolle critiques those who *semen* to be role models: the priests, the bishops, the enclosed, who, to all appearances, are living a holy life. What if they are also—on the inside—actually sinning and leading an unholy life? Rolle emphasizes that what happens in these situations is that the devil especially likes to pick apart the holy: "when he seth a man or a wommon amonge a þousand turne ham holy to God, [...] a thousand wiles he hath in what manere he may deceyue ham."[22] Further, Rolle writes, if he cannot make them publicly sin so that others can see them for what they are, "he begileth man so priuely þat þei can nat oft tymes fele þe trape þat hath take ham."[23] The devil then sets a trap that the holy person is not aware of—in other words they are living what they *think* is a holy life, but in truth they are ensnared in a devil's web. In order to live more harmoniously with God, this trap must be recognized. Rolle gestures toward the devil's traps as normative structures that render people false on the inside.

In order to see this deception, Rolle insists that the eremitic practitioner must understand the very nature of the snares. Again, Rolle wants the recluse to know themselves in order understand the part of them that is God. Many of these initial traps have to do with pride: "sum men he taketh with errour þat he putteth ham in; sum with synguler witte, whan he maketh ham wend þat þe thynge þat þei thynken or done is beste, and forthi thei wol no conseil haue of othre þat ben bettre and connyngre þan þei."[24] The nature of a sinful pride is that it cuts off relationships. The self is entirely centered on the *itself* and is not open. Further, this stain of pride attacks what should be beneficial spiritual activities. For example, Rolle writes that one could "delite in ham self of þe penaunce þat þei suffren."[25] Penance, abstinence, good works: for Rolle these are easily bent to sinful purposes as one takes improper delight in them, not for their outcomes, but because the solitary places themselves in the middle of the act, cutting God from the benefits.

Jesus cannot be loved "bot in clennesse."[26] This cleanness has to do with submitting the self to a process of understanding true Being. The original tempter came "in an angel of lighte" who "hideth yuel vndre þe liknesse of good."[27] For Rolle, the solitary's work is in being able to separate the "liknesse of good" from Real good. Thus, for Rolle, the

Real works beneath the level of appearance. And this "liknesse" can easily be faked, while the Real beneath is hidden from uncritical eyes. Rolle places the solitary in a unique position "the state þat þou art in, þat is solitude, þat is most able of al other to reuelacious of þe Holy Goste."[28] The solitary, though, has a certain predilection for privation; the ability to push the body to the limits is a hallmark of eremitic living. Rolle emphasizes that the solitary should not be excessive in their habits since this leads to further deception. If the solitary eats, drinks, and sleeps too well then it "makes vs slowe and cold in Goddis loue."[29] On the other hand, if there is too much penance the solitary risks "destrue" of the self.[30] In both cases, extremes lead to misconception and open the hermit to succumbing to deception. In the first case, easy living leads to too much comfort and thus a contentment in earthly pleasures resulting in a distancing from God. In the second case, bodily punishment leads to an erasure of the body, a body that is necessary to live a contemplative life. A sense of competition develops using excessive ascetic practices—the solitary begins to pride themselves on their extremes and, thus, prove that these practices are not for God, but, rather are done out of their own excessive sense of self.

Queer Time and Space

The excessive sense of self is linked to sin as a condition that separates the hermit from God. The eremitic self, the thinghood that is revealed in the tension between soul and body, stages the site from which the "*what is*" must be asked. Rolle's concern with solitude, with *sitting*, will be further addressed later as it is connected to a reorienting of the senses. For now, I want to focus on the queer space of the body and soul in a queer time.[31] Rolle writes, "I know þat þi lif semeth yeuen to þe service of God. þan is hit sham to þe, bot if þou be as good, or bettre, within in þi soule, as þou art semynge at þe syght of men. Therfor turne þi þoȝt perfitly to God, as hit semeth þat þou hast þi body."[32] For, Rolle, then, even if the solitary is identified—bodily—as someone whose spiritual practices are strong, it does not guarantee that they are actually living a true eremitic life devoted to God. Therefore, the hermit must bend both to God, aligning the soul with the body. It is noteworthy that Rolle queers the relation between body and soul; usually it is the body that leads the soul astray. In this text it is the body that leads the soul to the good. The soul is the truth teller, but it is also where falseness festers. One has to clean the soul to love.

For Rolle, the concept of "perfit love" indicates the alignment of body and soul in space. In order to achieve this, the solitary must also contemplate time. The solitary must keep four things in mind:

> on is þe mesure of þi life here, þat so short is þat vnnethe is oght; for we lyve bot in a point [...]. Anoþer is vncerteyntee of oure endynge; for we wot neuer whan we shall dye [...]. The þrid is þat we shal answare before þe rightuous juge of al þe tyme þat we han had here: how we haue lyved, whate oure occupacioun hath bene and whi [...]. The forth is þat we þynke how mych ioy is þat þay shal haue, þe which lesteth in Go[ddis] love to har endynge.[33]

Not only does the solitary need to think of their life as a point—to reveal themselves within the unfurling of eternity, but the solitary is encouraged to see their life moving into eternity. It is in the hermit's queer orientation to time and their activity of life in which various points of time overlap. As William Connolly writes, "a world of becoming—consisting of multiple temporal systems, many of which interact, each with its own degree of agency—is a world in which changes in some systems periodically make a difference to the efficacy and direction of others."[34] Rolle asks the solitary to consider an ending and a continuing, a world of eremitic time. There is a layer of time beneath that of the flow of life. In this way, Rolle sets up the contemplative life as a revelation: it will need to be revealed, accounted for at the time of judgment, but the contemplative, as a way to make sense of the point of time they currently occupy, will also set themselves into an eternal future. In this way, Connolly's systems of time begin to bump into one another. The "uncerteynte" of the ending of life is countered by the comfort of being "breþere and felewes with angels and holy men, louynge and hauynge, praising and seynge þe kynge of joy in þe fairheed and shynynge of his mageste."[35] The nature of time is both finite—life, narration of that life—and eternal—love of God, joys of heaven. But, the contemplative cannot have one without the other. Rolle's queer temporality takes account of time in various directions.

In *The Cloud of Unknowing*, the relationship between contemplative and God is experienced in darkness: "for yif euer schalt thou fele Him or see Him, as it may be here, it behoveth alweis be in this cloude and in this derknes."[36] Despite his admonition against metaphorical language, this metaphor indicates the *Cloud*-author's apophatic language; the mystical experience of the contemplative cannot be connected to anything known through ordinary sense experience. The oft-repeated passage of putting a cloud of unknowing "bitwix thee and thi God"[37] indicates that the *Cloud*-author sees the contemplative as one who is below his God, and the best way to realize the contemplative life is through a process of unknowing. Yet, he warns, this is not a real cloud, but a cloud of unknowing. His desire to limit language often empties the language of meaning. How are readers supposed to understand a cloud of unknowing without thinking of a cloud? Anytime there is any real sensory experience, the *Cloud-author* is immediately distrustful, admonishing his contemplative readers to "bewar in this werk, and travalyle not in thi wittes ne in this ymaginacion or no wise."[38] For the *Cloud*-author and his audience of contemplatives, God is the unknowable and also the un-experienced, at least through the senses.

It is very clear from the above passages that the *Cloud*-author attempts an apophatic language that asks the reader to think beyond figurative language. Yet, this method of thinking about spirituality and the relationship between the contemplative and God contrasts starkly with the work of Rolle. Where the *Cloud*-author uses cloud imagery to underscore unknowing, Richard Rolle's reference to clouds involves God actively spreading a cloud within the contemplative. Rolle writes of Psalm 105:39 in this way: "It is said of such *He has spread a cloud* (obviously a cloud of divine grace) *for a covering* (from carnal lust, by the fire of everlasting love) *and fire to give light* (within their mind) *in the night* (of this life); and all this lest they should be taken captive by the attraction of empty beauty."[39] From this brief overlap of images, one can see that whereas the *Cloud*-author insists on putting a cloud of unknowing between the contemplative and God, Rolle's emphasis, even in his exegesis, is exploring how God is present in the space of the soul. For Rolle the cloud is a space-maker spreading love and light within the hermit. There is no distance as such, and as I will demonstrate, much of Rolle's work is an attempt to discover and recover the space for God in the soul. Rather than focus on outward practices or outward spaces as we find in other texts concerned with solitaries, such as the *Ancrene Wisse* or *The Cloud of Unknowing*, Richard Rolle's orienting of contemplative living involves readying the heart and soul for God to become more legible in the space in which they *already* dwell and thus explore the colocality of an eremitic self and God.

While we can easily read *The Cloud of Unknowing* as being in opposition to Richard Rolle in terms of the *importance* of the senses, Rolle, too, is careful to be nuanced about the role of the senses in contemplation as is evident in his discussion of the "eye of the heart" and the space it occupies within the soul. Critics have pointed out the important aspects of the "eye of the heart." Louise Nelstrop, for example, writes that the "eye of the heart" is an important event in Rolle's eremitic schema, one that is often underplayed: "there is a clear relationship between the opening of the eye of the heart and mental or internal stability of thought [...]. Rolle argues that it is as one's thoughts become fixed on God that the heart is set alight, heaven is opened, and the soul enters into contemplation."[40] Nicholas Watson, too, notes the "eye of the heart" as an aspect of Rolle's description of contemplative life describing it "as a sign of blessings to come, but is otherwise of insignificant experience."[41] Whether the "eye of the heart" is central or insignificant to Rolle's mystical theology is clearly up for debate; however, the spatiality of the eye of the heart is hard to miss. The eye of the heart *within* the contemplative is a kind of sight and, for Rolle, a way that the contemplative discovers his inner soul and is afforded a view of heaven itself. The "eye of the heart" is an essential element of the hermit's discovery of the space and time of the soul. The opening of the body reveals the eremitic ontology of the body previously undiscovered as it connects the now with a divine future as it is situated within a recoverable within.

In *The Form of Living*, Rolle outlines the contemplative life as divinely inspired with God speaking to the heart, first, and then its eye opening. God inspires the hermit to forsake the world, and eventually He "ledeth ham by ham on, and speketh to her herte."[42] God then "setteh" the contemplative, until eventually, after many tribulations, the eyes of their souls are opened: "þe eigh of har soule þe yate of heuyn, so þat þe eigh loke in to heuyn."[43] As the eye of the heart is opened, it is important to emphasize that this is a heart that sees from within. As I will discuss below, Rolle warns that the outward senses can mislead, yet, Rolle here includes the act of seeing because it is a seeing born out of contemplation, born of the solitary life-space; when the eye is opened, the fire of love then comes into the heart. Deception is clearly recognized with the divinely inspired scopic power of the eye of the heart.

Sight is important in another way in Rolle's work, as it is an active function of the eremitic life itself. Contemplation is a kind of seeing for Rolle: "contemplacioun is a sight, and þai seth in to heuyn with har gostly eigh."[44] But, it is important to understand his complex spatiality; contemplative sight comes from *within* and it is only from within that the contemplative will see into heaven. Rolle describes how the hermit must open themselves in order to see outwardly. When they have finally reached the point of greatest contemplation, they are able to see with a spiritual sight into that which was most hidden from them.

Richard Rolle's concept of the inner self is not only a site for the seat of God, but, most interestingly, as a space that already exists within the contemplative. The discovery of this inner space is a move to join inner and outer worlds. Rolle uses spatial rhetoric to articulate the contemplative's need for space—he indicates this in many ways but is most clear in the way he describes the turning of the body to God and the way in which the solitary life is a turning inward. Rolle's spatial methodology, the turning to an inner heart to which Jesus can rest, contrasts greatly with that of the *Cloud*. In the *Cloud*-author's descriptions, there will always be unknowing between God and the contemplative, while Rolle emphasizes the openness of the contemplative with God through cultivating the queer capability of the space within the body through the power of the eye of the heart.

In the *Incendium*, Rolle validates the role of the hermit in medieval life because of its situatedness in a wilderness marked by queer time and space. Rolle rationalizes the solitary life by using this passage from Job: "Who hath sent the wild ass free? Or who hath loosed the bands of the wild ass? Whose house I have made the wilderness, and the barren land his dwelling?"[45] The wilderness, Rolle writes, is directly connected to the solitary for it means "'quietness of heart' because holy hermits, away from tumult and town, experience sweetness with a clear conscience through the generosity of Christ [...] And though in the body they suffer hardship and adversity, yet in the spirit they maintain a constant harmony and fervour."[46] Rolle divides body and soul: one will experience tribulation, but the spirit will experience joy. On the outside, there is trouble; however, the contemplative experiences a great peace within. Later, the outward tribulations are rewarded in heaven:

> Because for the sake of the Saviour the holy hermit has made solitude his home, in heaven he will receive a dwelling, golden and glistening, and in the midst of the angelic orders. Because for love of his Creator he dressed in filthy rags, his Maker will clothe him in eternal splendor [...] he who has loved so ardently; he is caught up to that eternal hall, and honoured in the most splendid fashion, to sit on high with the seraphim.[47]

These are themes that Rolle will repeat. The contemplative will dwell in solitude; they will then be rewarded by dwelling with angelic multitudes.

The contemplative will wear filthy clothes but be rewarded with fine clothes in heaven. The inside/outside schema he develops hinges on the hermit's disregard for outward things, settling into a queer temporality as the now becomes a reoccurring echo of the future.

Rolle combines place (heart/wilderness) and position (sitting) to indicate that out of this confluence *fervor* and *canor* will arise: "I call it fervor when the mind is truly ablaze with eternal love, and the heart similarly feels itself burning with a love that is not imaginary but real [...]. I call it song when there is in the soul, overflowing and ardent, a sweet feeling of heavenly praise, when thought turns into song [...]."[48] The wilderness is a space where the event of conversation between solitary and God occurs; Rolle writes "in the solitude they meet more openly, for there the Beloved speaks to the heart. It is very much like the bashful lover who will not embrace his girl in public or even greet her as a friend."[49] In the open, in public spaces, God will not speak with the contemplative. However, in the wilderness, in the quiet, in the solitary place, God speaks to the soul, piercing it with conversation. In the solitude of place, the contemplative finds itself opened.

Rolle is not only concerned with the orientation of the body in space, but also the space within the body where God resides. Again, there is a certain ambivalence to physical spaces as he writes, autobiographically, that even though he was raised above earthly things, he still "conformed quite properly to those with whom I was living lest I should invent a sanctity where none existed."[50] Although Frances Comper writes that Rolle is "carried away by excess of love, [he] never forgets the earth from which he has taken flight,"[51] Rolle discusses how he had reached a point of hating filth, vanity of words, and superfluous meat, even though he was still fed in "rich men's houses"[52] He defends his use of these normative luxuries by suggesting that he was only able to partake of the food offered because he had already reached a state where spaces of the world did not matter. God works in his soul "[...] I have never ceased to love solitude, and have chosen to live apart from men, as far as the needs of the body allow—and I have been continually upheld by him who I love."[53] Rich houses, solitary wilderness—this reveals a tension as it pertains to dwellings, for at the same time that Rolle praises the stability of place, he realizes that the only truly stable space is the space within. This tension speaks to a contemplative problem going back to the Benedictines, as well. Peter-Damian Belisle writes that although desert imagery appears in the work of Cistercians like Bernard of Clairvaux who strongly influence the writings of Richard Rolle, "the Cistercians were Benedictines and definitely cenobitic trying as much as possible to be self-sustaining and self-contained. What 'desert' they lived in was the spiritual desert of temptation and struggle."[54] We can see this reflected in the tension between Rolle and his audience; he struggles to create a contemplative space, a desert where there is none, where he can struggle alone. He attempts to live in metaphor.

What I have outlined in this section are the ways in which Rolle approached queer time and space. From the home of Job, to the wilderness, to the Dalton's manor house, Rolle realized that, in order to sit properly, he needed a space, but the space that mattered the most was the seat of the heart, the place where God would sit within the contemplative. It is in opening the inside to the divine that a queer time between futurity and the now is forged. Even though his worldly dwelling is his flesh, he longs for a release from how the flesh is configured, "though I am now physically sitting in solitary state, I seem to be seated in Paradise, there singing sweetly my song of love for the joys my Beloved has given me."[55] The passing forth will occur from the soul opening, but only when the solitary is able to understand the within and be stable there. The inner opening is where they must focus their attention, for as much as Rolle struggled with physical spaces, he was most interested in defining the time and space of the soul as an integral aspect of the hermit's ontology.

Kinds of Stability

Although other contemplative works denigrate the body to such an extent that the body is an unfortunate obstacle and only worthy of purgation, Rolle emphasizes a certain kind of bodily configuration as the source of contemplative power, hence his emphasis on living *appropriately*. The ideal of living appropriately is made clear in his discussion of being "right disposed."[56] Being "right disposed" means to understand the character of the human being: "what thynge fileth a man [. . .]. What maketh hym clene [. . .] what holdeth hym in clennesse [. . .] what þynge draweth hym for ordeyne his wille al to Goddis wille."[57] Again, we return to the concept of knowing oneself, but also as is indicated in the use of the third-person "hym," Rolle seems to be widening his reach and suggesting an anthropology that guides the contemplative: what constitutes this "hym?"

It is in this "hym" that Rolle addresses the nature of eremitic being in the relation between the heart, the mouth, and the deed. These sites of the body are vulnerable to sin and must be carefully guarded and made right, but they also indicate the queerness of eremitic being in its emphasis on refiguring the body of the hermit. These three act as poles in which Rolle's ontology is based: the heart, mouth, and deed are points in the life of the hermit that cause perturbations in the local—they uncouple the hermit from one environment (the deceptive world) into another (the eremitic site) or, if not properly aligned with God, they recouple the hermit to the world. In other words, the heart, mouth, and deeds *are* eremitic, because through them that being is constituted.

Rolle is concerned with how the heart connects with the divine and how it is connected to the community. Rolle writes that the sins of the heart consist of "il thoghtis, il delites, assent to syn, desire of il, wikked wille [...]," etc.[58] The heart is not only connected to emotional stuntedness, for example, "il deed, il loue, errour, fleishly affeccioun to þi frendes or to others þat þou louest" but also poor thinking, "vnstablenesse of thoght, pyne of penaunce, ypocrisi, loue to plese men, dred to displese ham, sham of good deed."[59] Thoughts and emotions are situated in the heart, and this catalogue of problems that Rolle reports indicates both the inability to align the heart with God as in the "assent to sin" and also an unhealthy relationship with the community and the self. Being too concerned with pleasing or displeasing others not only leads one astray from the ability to love God, but also leads one to be ashamed of one's good deeds. Earlier in this litany of sins, Rolle writes of "perplexite (þat is dout what is to do, what nat, forr every man oweth to be sikyre what he shal do and what he shal leue)."[60] The idea of "perplexite," this inability to decide, speaks to the bent nature of the self—it is being upset by a lack of center, of distraction that clouds the contemplative being.

If the sins of the heart indicate the ways in which the emotions and thoughts can ground the hermit in the wrong path, the sins of mouth indicate the public nature of the contemplative being. The environment of the hermit is important in that Rolle's text is attempting to move, to cause vibrations in the hermit, but the hermit is never apart from a wider community. Rolle recognizes that the hermit can never be completely severed from the world—as was indicated earlier, the body is the anchor—however, he works to change the track of the hermit so that they move toward God. Not only is it sinful to slander God or swear in his name but also to "gruch ayayns God for any anguys or noy or tribulacioun þat may befalle in erth [...],"[61] which indicates a lack of God's being on the part of the community. To "gouch" would imply that God does not know what It is doing, and, thus putting oneself at odds with God's will. God is no longer part of the network if It is somewhere else acting apart from the community. And, in this, Rolle reveals how queer the hermit can be. The hermit in the community is committed to a love that reveals a gentle friendship. They model themselves on God's encompassing love and not on normative concerns such as money or station.

The Form of Living is concerned with deception—the world that presents itself is a kind of disjointedness that *produces* the hermit. The concern in Rolle's eremitic ontology is what kinds of objects need to be in existence in order for the contemplative to exist. One key to eremitic relations is the attitude toward neighbors. The contemplative must avoid discord with the neighbors: "manacynge, sowynge of discord, tresone, fals witnes, il consail [...] turne good deeds to il for to make ham be holden il þat don ham (we owen for to lap oure neghbors dedes in þe best and not in þe worst)."[62] Rolle's capacious attitude toward neighbors, to hold them to the best intentions is a way to "uncouple" from judgment. As Žižek remarks, "the person who mistrusts his others is, paradoxically, in his very cynical disbelief, the victim of the most radical self-deception [...] the true believer [...] sees Goodness in the other where the other himself is not aware of it."[63] To place oneself in judgment of the neighbor's deeds or even to cause political (treason, false witness) problems with one's mouth proves that one is out of joint with being. Rolle has eschewed biological family structures to forge an eremitic community based in nonjudgmental grace and open love.

Finally, Rolle describes the problems of the sins of deeds. Rolle begins with a roll call of the various ways one can break the law of the Ten Commandments. These are direct acts against the Law, but, again, Rolle widens actions to describe community disharmony. Rolle is critical of hurting "any man in his body or in his goodes or in his fame [...], withhold necessaries fro þe body or yeve hit outrage [...], feynynge of moore good þan we haue to seme holier or connynger or wiser þan we bene."[64] Rolle speaks to the way that the elements of God, self, and community constitute the ontology of the hermit. It is of interest to note not only the power that the hermit-contemplative has in his community but also the political nature that it can hold. Rolle warns against treason and false witness, and also harming goods. There is a sense that Rolle has cast a wide net—these are the problems of every *body* and, thus, his queer anthropology studies human failing. However, Rolle is suggesting that human being is not a failed case, rather that normative structures lend themselves to judgment, to a turning on the community itself. The normative nature of the human simply needs to be queered:

> the thynges þat clenseth vs of þat filthede ben þre, ayeyns þay þre manere of synnes. þe first is sorowe of hert ayeynes þe synnes of thought; and þat behoueth to be perfite, þat þou wolt neuer syn moor [...]. The tother is shrift of mouth again þe syn of mouth and þat shal be hasted withouten delaynge, naked withouten excusynge, and entier without departynge, as for to tel a syn to oon prest and aþother to anothere; sey al þat þou wost to oon, or al is nat worth. The þrid is satisfaccoun, þat hath þre parties, fastynge, prier, and almysdede; nat þat doth þe wronge and pray for ham, and enfourme ham how þay shal do þat ben in point to perisshe.[65]

The advice that Rolle provides here is in protracting the body into a truth. The mouth should be given "shrift" but also made transparent. Rather than try to spread around one's sins to multiple priests so that no one has any clear idea of the depth of sin, one should tell them all to one so as to avoid shallowness. The depth of the person needs to be explored rather than taking comfort in mere law and rules.

The contemplative's will and God's will are not initially in accord. The contemplative must be shaped to accord with God; to do that the contemplative must act. Rolle frames these actions in thinking. Origen, in discussing how to interpret scripture, writes, "what also needs to be said about what kind of intelligence we must have to understand fully the discourse stored in the earthen treasure (see 2 Cor. 4:7) of ordinary speech, that is, a letter legible to anyone who chance to read it and audible by the sound of the sensible word to all who attend with their bodily ears? Someone who is going to comprehend it accurately must be able to say with truth, 'We have the intelligence of Christ, so that we know the things graciously given to us by God' (1 Cor. 2:16 and 12)."[66] Rolle also recommends three kinds of thinking: the contemplative should first heed the "ensample of holy men and women."[67] These men and women are marked as holy by their devotion to God. Rolle writes that by imitating them on earth "we mowe be with ham in heuyn."[68] In turning to past practices, Rolle situates the hermit in a kind of queer time. By bringing the hagiographical into the contemplative's current being and connecting them with an indeterminate future—this moment is layered with what spools from it—Rolle places the contemplative into the flow of eternity that no longer worries about a physical situatedness. The nostalgic queer acts in the now to connect the past and the future in ever-spiraling loops.

The next line of thinking is contemplating the goodness of God. God rejects no one. Anyone who will "cum to his mercy" will be accepted.[69] Rolle writes that the contemplative should wonder at the "ioy of þe kingdom of heuyn."[70] In contemplating heaven and the joys therein, there is a level of excess, there is more than enough to contemplate: more "þan tonge can tel or hert may thynke or eygh may see or eere may hire."[71] Heaven overloads the senses in this form of contemplation. This level of contemplation will bring the contemplative out of their own rootedness of their sense; the joys of heaven are more than one could say or hear or think.

Rolle sets up a dichotomy of life in heaven and hell. In hell the fire burns so much that nothing lives but for God's will; in heaven, the joy is so much that the lover would die for joy if not for Jesus' goodness: "þat wil þat his louers be lyvynge euer in bliss, as in rightwisness wil þat al þat lovet hyn nat be euer lyvynge is fyre."[72] In both eternal places one wants to die because of the excess—an unendurable pain or perpetual, orgasmic joy. But, it is only the will of God that *keeps* one suffering and one joyful. There is no difference between the two eternal places in terms of *eros*, excess, and saturation. The nature of the soul is tethered to the problem of the body for Rolle. For the soul lives, but only in a way that God touches it. In other words, much like the contemplative's final step in which God wills whether to grant the contemplative a vision of the future (and present) joy, so will the soul be eternally alive to pain or joy based on God's will. The contemplative must take the first steps to be within God's will. The nature of contemplative being is based on the contemplative's will in so much as the contemplative must recognize, approach, and act to be a part of God's will. Only then can imitation produce fruit as the contemplative will grow and realize their capaciousness toward the community.

To "dispose þi lyf" is to realize God's will.[73] In other words, eremitic being takes a thinking through as to how to adjust, how to open oneself to God's being rather than structures surrounding the hermit. The contemplative wants more, what Rolle calls "sum special point."[74] The "point" is in understanding the nature of love and opening the self to that love. Rolle explores the nature of love through the concept of song: "for he þat mych loueth, hym lust oft to synge of his loue [...] I languysshe for loue."[75] This act of languishing is a response to the excessive, contemplative gift: "þe special yift of þe þat ledeth solitary life is for loue Ihesu Criste."[76]

For Rolle, this gift is both excessive and difficult to navigate. The contemplative acts, and in the performance the love of Jesus becomes legible. However, there are objections. Could one not say they love God if they hold the Commandments? This kind of rule-following is not enough for Rolle and he brackets those who stop there: "bot al men þat kepeth his byddynge kepeth nat also his consail, and al þat doth his consail is not as fulfilled of þe swetnesse of his loue, ne feleth nat þe fyre of loue brennynge his herte."[77] Rolle sets up a hierarchy of contemplation: those angels and men and women who love God more will be in proximity to God in heaven, those who love him less will be in a "lower ordre."[78] The burning of love found in the fire-heart is key for Rolle (as we will see in the next chapter); if one does not feel the fire of the love then one is not loving enough and "litel is þi delite."[79]

Contemplatives must immerse themselves in thinking about God night and day. Rolle writes that at every bite of food, every morsel, one should be thinking about the Passion—but not only at that moment—even before and after. Rolle adds nuance here, writing that whatever devotional idea one has in the heart is good, but he warns, be careful of relying on quantity. It does not matter how much one says, rather "how welle, þat þe eigh of þy hert be ever upward, and þi thought on þat þat þou seist, as ych as þou may."[80] The eye of the heart is turned upward—the heart contains both eye and the seat of thought for Rolle—the contemplative's being is seated in a stable space with God.

An Ethos of Love

In Patrick Cheng's estimation there are many kinds of queer Christologies. As he describes one such Christology, the Self-Loving Christ avoids the sin of shame and "has sufficient self love to persist in his ministry and vocational calling;" it is "not possible to love another authentically without also having a healthy amount of love for oneself."[81] As has been discussed, one of Rolle's concerns in both the *Incendium Amoris* and *The Form of Living* is the love the hermit-contemplative must cultivate. This includes the love and understanding of the self for the within in which God is seated; how can one be ashamed (and thus be in a perpetual state of sin-as-separation) of a self that is in constant, but unrealized, contact with God?

The concept of stability for Rolle is important because it leads to the ability to love. However, stability can mean two things in Rolle's work. In one way, it is a (failed) attempt to find physical stability, a place to pray. In another way, it means inner stability, a way to make evident a place for God to sit in the heart. It is this inner stability that receives the most emphasis in Rolle's discussions. In *The Form of Living*, Rolle writes, "If þou wil be wel with God, and haue grace to reul þi lif and cum to þe ioy of loue, þis name Ihesu fest hit so faste in þi hert, þat it cum never out of þi þought."[82] Rolle's admonition to never let Christ out of the contemplative's thoughts leads to an overcoming of the separation of sin so that the contemplative lives with hope. This requires a reorientation with the world as it is. The unity that Rolle desires for the contemplative is explained as healing all wrongs within: "If þou thynk Ihesu continuely, and hold hit stably, hit purgeth þi syn and kyndels thyn hert [...] hit woundethin loue, fulfilleth in charite, hit chaseth þe deuyl and putteth out drede, hit openeth heuyn and maketh a contemplatif man."[83] The stability that Rolle wishes for the contemplative encompasses the ability to focus on Christ and to reveal what is closed to the non-contemplative. To open heaven, to open the inner door and keep it open, is Rolle's goal.

From this discussion of a perpetual holding of Christ within, Rolle moves to a discussion of the "what" and the "where" of Love. Rolle redirects the contemplative reader from what practices they should enact to a discussion of exactly what they are holding in stability. Rolle writes, "Bot now may þou ask me and say: 'þou spekest so mych of loue, tel me, what loue is, and whare hit it is [...]'."[84] In answering these questions, Rolle invokes concepts of joining and space to make clear the "hard questyons" raised. Love is a "brenynge desire in God [...]. Loue is a life coupelynge togiddre þe louynge to þe loued."[85] We can contrast these questions with those raised by the *Cloud*-author. The *Cloud*-author writes, "But now thou askest me and seiest: 'How shcal I think on Himself, and what is Hee?' And to this I cannot answere thee bot thus: 'I wote never'."[86] The rhetorical similarity is striking, as both Rolle and the *Cloud*-author imagine an interlocutor who seeks guidance. Yet, for the *Cloud*-author, the answer is negative—I know not. These questions lead to a plea to "chese to my love that thing that I cannot think."[87] Rolle, is more generous to his interlocutors and attempts answers.

For Rolle, Love is like a sticky substance fusing the wills of the contemplative and God. Rolle returns to the idea that the contemplative life is the place of Love and that Love is what makes one a hermit-contemplative. In answering the second question, Rolle locates Love and warns against outward showings of religious belief: "loue is in þe hert and in þe wil of þe man, nat in is hand ne in his mouth; þat is to say nat in his werke bot in his soule. For many speketh good and doth good, and loueth nat God [...]."[88] It is easy to deceive oneself about how one loves. For Rolle, Love is in the soul, in the heart—for Rolle they are the same. In *Incendium Amoris*, Rolle writes in a similar vein: "the nature of love is that it is diffusive, unifying, and transforming."[89] Love is not in outward things—not in doing or saying. Here we begin to see Rolle concentrating on the inner life of the contemplative and disregarding the rituals that are commonly categorized as (normative) religious acts. In encouraging Margaret Kirkby to disregard outer acts, Rolle encourages the development of an inner soul that loves. Rolle's location of Love within the heart and the framing of Love as a desire, an erotic longing between the contemplative and God, conceptualizes Love as the *ethos* of the heart as it expresses the divine in the world.

To open oneself to Love is the most difficult aspect of Rolle's ontology to experience. If the flesh is separated by sin, if the hermit is not open to loving the neighbor as oneself, if the seat of the heart is not prepared, Love will be impossible to practice or experience. The contemplative's becoming toward God is located in a matrix that is the nature of love. Rolle's discussion of love involves two dimensions. First, Rolle addresses degrees of love. These degrees of love are levels to which the contemplative must attain or "win"[90] as they mature. The other dimension of love that Rolle discusses is Love itself—the being of Love. If *The Form of Living* is a guide for contemplative to turn their life to God, Rolle's ontology is in the nature of Love itself. In a Socratic-like dialogue, Rolle begins with three questions: what is love?; where is love?; and how do I love?

The three degrees of love are "insuperabile," "inseparabile," and "synguler." The contemplative achieves "insuperabile" love when the love is stable in the face of all obstacles. In marriage-like language, Rolle describes the love as stable whether "in ese or in anguys, in heel or in sekeness, so þat þe þhynke þat þou will nat for þe world, to haue hit withouten end, wreth God oo time."[91] This love conforms to Rolle's wish for stability of heart. This is the foundational love that the other forms of love rest upon. Rolle writes further that this is a good love to have, but it is even better for the contemplative if they can move onto other types of love.

If "insuperabile" love is a foundation for the heart, "inseparabile" love is marked by an internal oneness. *Insuperabile* love is threatened by the external, so that for Rolle love is truly *inseparabile* if it will not bow to anything that happens externally to the contemplative. *Inseparabile* is characterized by colocality with Jesus. The contemplative is fastened to the thought of Jesus so that "þi thought and þi myght is so hooly, so entirely and so perfitly fasted, set, and stablet in Ihesu Criste þat þi þoght cometh neuer of hym, neuer departeth fro hym."[92] The prepositions "of" and "fro" indicate the contemplative's unity with their self in Jesus. The only time the contemplative's self departs from Jesus is in sleep, but immediately upon waking the contemplative returns to Jesus-thought. There is a singularity in this thinking as the contemplative is aligned with Jesus; however, Rolle leaves his longest discussion for the third kind of love: *synguler*.

"Synguler" love is the highest form of love that the contemplative can experience and it is marked by the feeling of fire that the contemplative experiences. As Rolles writes, this love "hath no pere."[93] The contemplative experiences solace and comfort from Jesus only and nothing else. For Rolle, Jesus and self are thoroughly intertwined and He is the sole sitter and occupier of the heart. The heart-fire that burns in the heart is erotic in that it is "so delitable and wonderful þat I can not tel hit."[94] The fire defies descriptions though it can be likened "as þou may fele þi fynger bren if þou put hit in þe fyre".[95] At this level the soul is Jesus-bound: "þe soul is Ihesu thynkynge, Ihesu desyrynge, only in coueitys of hym."[96] The gap between Jesus and the heart is lessened here—if there is a gap at all. The heart begins to embody Jesus, makes itself Jesus-like, as it burns, thinks, desires. The soul makes a final transformation when it becomes song.

The soul—in the midst of its desire for Jesus within, thinking of Jesus—becomes a song of Jesus. It is at this point that Rolle points out the contemplative will be overwhelmed to see Jesus and that the feeling of "deth swetter þan hony"[97] is proof the soul is secured to Him. The contemplative has passed from normative love to a love that has made that death sweet. But, despite this sweet death, Rolle indicates that along with song, it is here that the contemplative no longer "languishes," rather, it is here that the contemplative experiences the profound change of their body sleeping and the heart awake.

As Rolle points out, in the first two levels the contemplative languishes as it wants a cure from a sickness.[98] It is only in the third degree that the heart/soul is fulfilled like a "brennynge fyre, as þe nyghtgalle, þat loveth songe and melody [...]."[99] This soul is only comforted in song and so will sing for the rest of its days of Jesus. Rolle further wants to separate this song from regular every day singing. This genre of song is only experienced *at this level* of love. And, further, this love is a gift from God, it comes from heaven; when the contemplative has this song, all the songs of earth seem "bot sorowe and woo."[100]

These three levels of love act as a guide to what the contemplative is capable of experiencing. The ontology of love is different from a pure erotic love, though with its desire for Jesus and the need to not be separated from Him, there is an eroticism that Rolle will explore further in the lyrics and a centering of worship on the name of Jesus. Here Rolle's ontology is of a love that is out there for the contemplative to experience as long as they can see their relationship to the world clearly (and queerly). The world of some kinds of matter are a distraction that limits what the contemplative can experience—either by keeping them in the active path or keeping them at the lower levels of the love experience.

For Rolle, this ontology of love has another dimension, that of the Loved. The questions that Rolle poses at the end of *The Form of Living* create an ontology of God that suggest being, location, and connection between contemplative and God. For Rolle God contains Love: "love is a brennynge desire in God, with a wonderful delite and sikernesse. God is light and brennynge."[101] This love emanates out from God so that love becomes an object: "love is a *thynge* þrogh which God loveth vs, and loveth God, and every of vs other."[102] For Rolle, love is an aspect of thinghood by which God and contemplative touch. We can think of it as the object that Rolle is attempting to discover that changes shape, size, and dimension depending on who is touching it. It is the object that is the nexus. It "coupelynge togiddre þe louynge to þe loued."[103] Rolle separates Love from loving here—love is the object, something necessary in order to love. Love is a separate surface of God and it is that surface that the heart touches and loves God.

Love is, then, a turning. This object joins the contemplative with God. As Rolle writes, Love "clenseth þe soule, and delyveseth hit fro þe peyn of hol."[104] So, the nature of Love, the essence, is of a cleansing object, one that joins, saves, and centers loving. I imagine here Rolle holding up a crystal and turning it in his hand allowing each facet to catch the light. This Love, like the heart that I will discuss in the next chapter, is a centering object where love can be experienced; without it, there is no focus, no clear direction for the contemplative to go. The heart, Rolle remarks as he closes the discussion of this first question, is central, as well; the contemplative's "hert shal so bren in love þat hit shal be turned in to fire of love, and be as hit were al fyre, and he shal be so shynynge in vertuȝ þat in no part of hym [he] be darke in vices."[105] The contemplative's heart becomes fire. It is important to note, however, that the contemplative's being becomes the phenomenon of Love—God is fire; It is the burning—the true contemplative becomes like that God-object with light emanating from them, as well.

Love is found within the heart. Rolle locates love not in works—not in the "hand, ne in his mouth."[106] Works lead to flattery and the contemplative can be misled by works, so that they rest in their works assured by others that they are doing good. Again, Rolle warns his audience about those who "seemeth holy."[107] The deception of holiness covers over the lack of stability in those who devote themselves to garnering praise from others. Rolle insists that good works are truly good if they are based in thinking about and through God. Rolle further points out that no one can tell if he loves God: "then can on tel me if I loue God, for noght þat þay see me do."[108] There is a division between those who do good and those who do good based in love. However, as Rolle indicates human beings are unable to tell the difference. Love will continually work since it occupies the will "verraili, nat in werke bot as signe of loue."[109] Love is not found in the outward good works that are visible except as sign: "loue will nat be ydel."[110] Love here is located, then, in the heart and it is noteworthy that it emanates out only in significance. Love is behind good works, but it is not in the works themselves. One who is "possessed" by love will act out in goodness always, but the one who does good work is not necessarily occupied by love, especially if they act in order to get praise. For them, though Rolle does not say so explicitly, works and love are separate objects, only colliding in the true contemplative's environment. On the one hand, love is foundational for good works; on the other hand, good works can happen without love, though, the implication is that these works are not "best" practices. If love is the object, the mediator in relations that is found in the heart, the gift of good works passes through it, charging it with higher value. Without Love, as found in the one who seeks praise, the good work is cheapened by the giver, though the receiver still benefits from the gift (i.e., giving someone a blanket to keep them warm, even if one is doing it to receive praise, cheapens the giver's act but not the receiver's warmth).

In answering the question, "How does one love God?" Rolle further explores the nature of the will. The will must first be made meek: "he is stalworth that is meke, for al gostly streynth cometh of mekenesse."[111] The strength from humility argument that Rolle employs delivers the contemplative into the might of will that the contemplative will have as a heavenly reward: "þat þay may haue hit plenely in þe toþer."[112] A meek will overcomes even the devil; Rolle sees humility, not passivity, as stronger.

No matter what a person does on earth—fasting or suffering—without the meekness of will that is stable, for it is "nat stirred for any word þat men may say"[113]—they are unable to have Love. It is interesting to note on these last items that Rolle is critiquing traditional ascetic acts—fasting, suffering—as only a practice, not Love itself. This repeats his critiques of good works earlier reiterating that acts need Love as their intention.

The heart must also wisely love God. Wisdom consists of moving oneself away from the world. Those who are foolish "spend in coveitise and bisynesse about þe world."[114] Wisdom for Rolle most has to with object choice. A person who is unable to identify true value is unable to love wisely. For Rolle, those who love an apple rather than precious stones (in order to buy a castle), would appear as a fool.[115] Rolle, oddly, uses this extended metaphor to warn the contemplative not to be so concerned with the world. The contemplative's precious jewels, however, are "poverte and penaunce and gostly trauaille."[116] With these metaphorical jewels the contemplative can buy the kingdom of heaven. For Rolle wisdom—using the heart wisely—has to do more with turning the heart to God than solving real world problems. The wise heart knows where true value is: in recognizing the way a normative world distracts from loving God, and, thus, correcting the self from that distraction.

Finally, Rolle addresses the issue of the state of the contemplative: how must they *be* in order to love God? For Rolle, this has everything to do with the body; Rolle writes that "I have loued for to sit, for no penaunce ne for no fantasie 'þat' I would men spake of me, ne for no such þyng, bot only for I knewe þat I loued God more, and langer lested with me comfort of loue, than goynge or standynge or knelynge."[117] In sitting, Rolle is rested, able to focus, able to aim his "hert most vpward."[118] Rolle ends *The Form of Living* with this discussion of the sitting body—the experience of the body in contemplation and the reorienting of the senses is key to loving in stability. Thus, discovering the queer capabilities of the senses is an essential quality of eremitic being.

Eremitic ontology moves the contemplative to see the work and love of God in the world and within—the new capability of the body and soul are awakened with the touch of God. The deceptiveness of the world normalizes the senses of the hermit making God less legible, less touchable. This normalization must be overcome through the opening of the soul and the recognition of the multitude of Love. In the next chapter, we turn to the phenomenology of the sitting contemplative and the reorientation of the hermit's sense-world in order to see how Rolle's eremitic ontology allows the hermit to experiment with their senses, experience new phenomena, and forge new divine communities while realizing the queer capabilities of the eremitic body.

Notes

1. Lee Edelman, *No Future: Queer Theory and the Death Drive*. (Durham: Duke University Press, 2004), p. 5.
2. Linne Marie Tonstad, *God and Difference: The Trinity, Sexuality, and the Transformation of Finitude* (New York: Routledge, 2016), p. 291.
3. Marcella Althaus-Reid, *Indecent Theology: Theological Perversions in Sex, Gender, and Politics* (Routledge: New York, 2000), p. 127.
4. Kevin Hart, "Absolute Interruption: On Faith" in *Questioning God*. Ed. John D. Caputo, Mark Dooley, and Michael J. Scanlon. (Blooming: Indiana University Press, 2001), p. 194.
5. Elizabeth Stuart, "Sacramental Flesh" in *Queer Theology: Rethinking the Christian Body*. Ed. Gerard Loughlin. (Malden, MA: Blackwell, 2007), p. 65.
6. Richard Rolle, *The Form of Living. Richard Rolle: Prose and Verse*. EETS no. 293. Ed. S.J. Ogilivie-Thomson (Oxford: Oxford University Press, 1988), ll. 705–707.
7. Graham Ward, "Questioning God" in *Questioning God*. Ed. John D. Caputo, Mark Dooley, and Michael J. Scanlon. (Blooming: Indiana University Press, 2001), p. 279.
8. Ward, p. 280.
9. Ward, p. 280.
10. Ward, p. 282.
11. Slavoj Žižek, *The Fragile Absolute*. (London: Verso, 2000), p. 118.
12. Žižek, *The Fragile Absolute*, p. 119.
13. Žižek, *The Fragile Absolute*, pp. 119–120.
14. Susannah Cornwall, *Controversies in Queer Theology* (London: SCM Press, 2011), pp. 63–64.
15. For a discussion of the English prose work of Richard Rolle and its audience see Claire Elizabeth McIlroy, *English Prose Treatises of Richard Rolle* (Cambridge: D.S. Brewer, 2004).
16. See Patrick S. Cheng, *From Sin to Amazing Grace: Discovering the Queer Christ* (New York: Seabury, 2012). Cheng argues for a rethinking of sin within queer theology that is not a form of punishment but rather a sign of "immaturity" in the Christian's relationship with God. Thus, overcoming sin is a stage in spiritual development rather than an ongoing mortification.
17. Grace Jantzen, "Contours of a Queer Theology" in *Feminism and Theology*. Ed. Janet Martin Soskice and Diana Lipton. (Oxford: Oxford University Press, 2003), p. 344.
18. Jantzen, p. 51.

19. Rolle, *The Form of Living*, ll. 453–454.
20. Rolle's need for ontological prescription finds its counterpart in Heidegger's commentary on the relationship between object and hermeneutic: "the theme of this hermeneutical investigation is the Dasein which is in each case our own and indeed as hermeneutically interrogated with respect to and on the basis of the character of its being and with a view to developing in it a radical wakefulness for itself," (*Ontology—The Hermeneutics of Facticity*, p. 12). The wakefulness is what Rolle is addressing against the problem of deception. As Michel Foucault comments in his March 19, 1980 lecture on *The Government of the Living* in the context of Clement of Alexandria, "one knows oneself so that one can have access to knowledge of God, that is to say so that one can recognize what is divine in oneself, so that one can recognize the part or element in the soul that is of divine form, principle, origin, or at any rate in contact with God." Ed. Michael Senellart. (New York: Palgrave MacMillan, 2012), p. 253.
21. Rolle, *The Form of Living*, ll. 18–20.
22. Rolle, *The Form of Living*, ll. 21–25.
23. Rolle, *The Form of Living*, ll. 26–28.
24. Rolle, *The Form of Living*, ll. 29–32.
25. Rolle, *The Form of Living*, ll. 35–36.
26. Rolle, *The Form of Living*, l. 160.
27. Rolle, *The Form of Living*, ll. 182–184.
28. Rolle, *The Form of Living*, ll. 138–139.
29. Rolle, *The Form of Living*, l. 190.
30. Rolle, *The Form of Living*, l. 191.
31. For a discussion of Richard Rolle's spatial mysticism in a historical context see Carmel Bendon David, *Mysticism and Space: Spatiality in the Works of Richard Rolle, The Cloud of Unknowing Author, and Julian of Norwich*. (Washington, D.C.: The Catholic University of America Press, 2008).
32. Rolle, *The Form of Living*, ll. 233–236.
33. Rolle, *The Form of Living*, ll. 280–288 and ll. 297–298.
34. William E. Connolly, *A World of Becoming* (Durham: Duke University Press, 2011), p. 27.
35. Rolle, *The Form of Living*, ll. 299–301.
36. *The Cloud of Unknowing*, ed. Patrick J. Gallacher (TEAMS: Kalamazoo, 1997), p. 31.
37. *The Cloud of Unknowing*, p. 35.
38. *The Cloud of Unknowing*, p. 34.
39. Rolle, *The Fire of Love*, trans. Clifton Walters (Penguin: London, 1972), p. 68.
40. Louise Nelstrop, "The Merging of Eremitic and 'Affectivist' Spirituality in Richard Rolle's Reshaping of Contemplation." *Viator* 35 (2004): 298.

41. See Nicholas Watson, *Richard Rolle and the Invention of Authority* (Cambridge: Cambridge University Press, 1991), p. 67.
42. Rolle, *The Form of Living*, ll. 877–78.
43. Rolle, *The Form of Living*, ll. 884–85.
44. Rolle, *The Form of Living*, ll. 888–89.
45. Rolle, *The Fire of Love*, footnote 1, p. 86.
46. Rolle, *The Fire of Love*, p.87.
47. Rolle, *The Fire of Love*, p. 88.
48. Rolle, *The Fire of Love*, p. 89.
49. Rolle, *The Fire of Love*, p. 168.
50. *The Fire of Love*, p. 78.
51. Comper, p. 123.
52. Rolle, *The Fire of Love*, p. 142.
53. Rolle, *The Fire of Love*, p. 142.
54. Peter-Damian Belisle, *The Language of Silence: The Changing Face of Monastic Solitude* (Maryknoll, NY: Orbis, 2003), p. 106.
55. Rolle, *The Fire of Love*, p. 97.
56. Rolle, *The Form of Living*, l. 323.
57. Rolle, *The Form of Living*, ll. 323–327.
58. Rolle, *The Form of Living*, ll. 329–33.
59. Rolle, *The Form of Living*, ll. 340–42.
60. Rolle, *The Form of Living*, ll. 336–38.
61. Rolle, *The Form of Living*, ll. 352–53.
62. Rolle, *The Form of Living*, ll. 355–358.
63. Žižek, *The Fragile Absolute*, p. 119.
64. Rolle, *The Form of Living*, ll. 367–72.
65. Rolle, *The Form of Living*, ll. 399–410.
66. Origen, "Commentary on John, Book I," in *Origen*. Ed. Joseph W. Trigg. (London: Routledge, 1998), p. 109.
67. Rolle, *The Form of Living*, l. 470.
68. Rolle, *The Form of Living*, l. 472.
69. Rolle, *The Form of Living*, l. 474.
70. Rolle, *The Form of Living*, l. 476.
71. Rolle, *The Form of Living*, ll. 476–77.
72. Rolle, *The Form of Living*, ll. 480–82.
73. Rolle, *The Form of Living*, l. 485.
74. Rolle, *The Form of Living*, l. 486.
75. Rolle, *The Form of Living*, ll. 490–94.
76. Rolle, *The Form of Living*, l. 495.
77. Rolle, *The Form of Living*, ll. 496–99.
78. Rolle, *The Form of Living*, l. 504.
79. Rolle, *The Form of Living*, l. 507.

80. Rolle, *The Form of Living*, ll. 520–22.
81. Cheng, *From Sin to Amazing Grace*, p. 111.
82. Rolle, *The Form of Living*, ll. 610–12.
83. Rolle, *The Form of Living*, ll. 615–620.
84. Rolle, *The Form of Living*, ll. 626–27.
85. Rolle, *The Form of Living*, ll. 633–34, 636–37.
86. *The Cloud of Unknowing*, p. 36.
87. *The Cloud of Unknowing*, p. 36.
88. *The Form of Living*, ll. 678–80.
89. *The Fire of Love*, p. 101.
90. Rolle, *The Form of Living*, l. 525.
91. Rolle, *The Form of Living*, ll. 529–531.
92. Rolle, *The Form of Living*, ll. 538–540.
93. Rolle, *The Form of Living*, l. 550.
94. Rolle, *The Form of Living*, l. 556.
95. Rolle, *The Form of Living*, l. 555.
96. Rolle, *The Form of Living*, ll. 556–557.
97. Rolle, *The Form of Living*, l. 562.
98. Rolle, *The Form of Living*, l. 567.
99. Rolle, *The Form of Living*, ll. 571–572.
100. Rolle, *The Form of Living*, l. 584.
101. Rolle, *The Form of Living*, ll. 633–635.
102. Rolle, *The Form of Living*, ll. 639–640, italics mine.
103. Rolle, *The Form of Living*, ll. 636–637.
104. Rolle, *The Form of Living*, l. 667.
105. Rolle, *The Form of Living*, ll. 674–677.
106. Rolle, *The Form of Living*, l. 679.
107. Rolle, *The Form of Living*, l. 682.
108. Rolle, *The Form of Living*, ll. 698–699.
109. Rolle, *The Form of Living*, l. 700.
110. Rolle, *The Form of Living*, l. 702.
111. Rolle, *The Form of Living*, ll. 709–709.
112. Rolle, *The Form of Living*, ll. 729–730.
113. Rolle, *The Form of Living*, l. 722.
114. Rolle, *The Form of Living*, ll. 738–739.
115. Rolle, *The Form of Living*, ll. 739–741.
116. Rolle, *The Form of Living*, ll. 742–743.
117. Rolle, *The Form of Living*, 829–831.
118. Rolle, *The Form of Living*, 833.

CHAPTER 3

The Phenomenology of the Open Body

> *So, if phenomenology is to attend to the background, it might do so by giving an account of the conditions of emergence for something, which would not necessarily be available in how that thing presents itself to consciousness.*
>
> —Sarah Ahmed, *Queer Phenomenology*

Abstract Richard Rolle's phenomenology explores the mystical event as enacted on the body of the hermit. In the act of narrating his experience, Rolle relates the preparation of the body for mystical experience by emphasizing its queer possibilities. By placing the body beyond normative sense structures, the body opens itself to the queer possibilities of experiencing the divine. Rolle orients the senses to the experience of fire, sweetness, and song as a way to unpack the queer touch of God on the eremitic body.

Keywords Phenomenology · *Fervor* · *Dulcor* · Senses · Mystical language

Chapter 2 described Richard Rolle's eremitic ontology. In resisting the easy categorization of eremitic being, Rolle puts forth a queer Christian identity, negotiating an inner stability, always in the process of self-creation. He reinforces the concerns of hermit-being through a focus on Love, loving, being, space, and time. This chapter relates his ontological openness to a rethinking of the phenomenology of mystical experience through queer bodies and experiences. Rolle's phenomenology is concerned with orientation, opening the body and questioning any fixed nature of the human senses in the moment of the divine caress.

© The Author(s) 2017
C.M. Roman, *Queering Richard Rolle*, The New Middle Ages,
DOI 10.1007/978-3-319-49775-4_3

By emphasizing seated meditation, the fiery heart, and the immersion of sweetness, Rolle opens the body for God's indwelling. The divine touch manifests its presence in three phenomenal realms: fire (*fervor*), sweetness (*dulcor*), and song (*canor*). This chapter deals with the first two phenomenon and leaves *canor* for a deeper exploration in Chapter 4. Rolle's theology attends to the revelation of a queer hermit, one that lives without a center, challenging to a Christian identity solely focused on law and penitence rather than mystical immersion. As God and the *becoming*-hermit touch, they each exhibit surfaces and depths, and Rolle meditates on the ways in which the eremitic body defies sensual limitations.

Rolle then constructs eremitic identity as vibrating between three poles, the fire or heat (*fervor*), the song (*canor*), and the sweetness (*dulcor*). The eremitic identity, framed through Rolle's experience is not only an attempt to reflect transcendent experience but throughout Rolle's work it is also a way to investigate and contemplate the hermit that is hidden, to make the hermit as *known* as possible while challenging the very horizon of that being. Following Augustine, Conor Cunningham emphasizes the recognition of being by God: "to be known by God is to *be*. Furthermore, creation preexists in the Word from eternity as its eternal utterance. Creation preexists in the Word in a manner which is superior to its mode of existence *in via* [...]."[1] As we have seen in Chapter 2, Rolle is searching for this Word by identifying normalizing deception. By utilizing the queer capability of his senses, Rolle is able to explore the divine touch. For Martin Heidegger, as we will see in Rolle, Christian life is not "straightforward, but is rather broken up: all surrounding-world relations must pass through the complex of enactment of having-become."[2] God touches; it is the hermit who needs to reciprocate by bending the body toward God through a performance that opens the self.

Phenomenology and Mysticism

One of the problems faced by medieval mystics, Richard Rolle included, is how to render into language the mystical experience filtered through the finite senses that have been then rendered queer by the divine touch, what M. F. Wakelin identified in Rolle as "the great gulf between his mind and the mind of the world."[3] Michael Warner encapsulates the queerness of religion when he writes, "religion makes available a language of ecstasy, a horizon of significance within which transgressions against the normal order of the world and the boundaries of the self *can be seen as good things*."[4] Warner points to how fundamental religiosity challenges the "most radical theories of sexual liberation" in seeking the "moral importance to self-dissolution."[5] In the case of Rolle's *Incendium Amoris*, his semi-autobiographical mystical work, Rolle attempts to capture his own mystical experience by pushing the boundaries of eremitic embodiment in acts of self-dissolution.

Rolle challenges embodied expectations in ways textual and sensual. Rolle's mysticism combines hagiography, exegesis, and protrepsis. As Eleanor Johnson points out protrepsis is "the literary modeling of ethical transformation in a main character who is also the narrator of the work."[6] He attempts to tell his story practicing protrepsis all the while creating an *aporia* in this text between identifying with his personal story and encouraging the reader to perform as hermit. Thus, Rolle queers his *individual* experience bending his story outward and encouraging the participation of others to come out, to bend their bodies in order to receive God's touch. In this way, Rolle is emphasizing a queer narrative theology that is *lived* experience, one that breaks down "traditionally fixed boundaries and categories"[7] of genre, theology, *via*, and narrative.

Rolle is concerned, then, with articulating how to speak about God, about experience, and about the body. Phenomenology places emphasis on the received experience that the subject perceives. As Annabelle Wilcox writes, "phenomenology [...] suggests a mutually constitutive relationship between the subject and object" where the body "can never be explored apart from its situation."[8] Rolle relates how both the touch and the phenomenon reciprocate a queerness that suggests new configurations of the body within the local divine moment. Rather than allow the reader to presume a normative, embodied nature of eremiticism, Rolle emphasizes his own body as a way to narrativize queer, eremitic embodiment. Thus, he encourages a queer community that exists in the space of readership across time and pages. In this way, the *Incendium Amoris* becomes an object (a mediator) aimed at making change in the world through the encouragement of queer, eremitic performance.

At the heart of Rolle's mystical experience is an attempt at community formation by modeling his life for readers as well as invoking queer histories involving "affective relations."[9] In thinking of the exchange of language between two or more entities, as such creating relationships, we can think of Rolle's narrative problem in terms of Jean-Luc Nancy's discussion of communication: "'language' is not an instrument of communication, and communication is not an instrument of Being; communication *is* Being, and Being *is*, as a consequence, nothing but the incorporeal by which bodies express themselves to one another *as such*."[10] In relating his mystical experience, Rolle is also queering the body's mode of communication in order to explore the mystical and eremitical being that constitutes a way of life.[11] Rolle's recounting of his experience, then, is a mystical phenomenology, an attempt to explore the embodied phenomenon of fire, sweetness, and song as divine relationship, while, at the same time refusing to foreclose for the reader the positive indeterminacy of divine queerness.

One way to bring phenomenology to the forefront of Rolle's work is to think about medieval cognition and its connection with sensuousness through John Duns Scotus.[12] Scotus is a major influence on medieval mystical literature, though his connection and influence on Rolle is little discussed. Conor Cunningham frames Scotus' description of cognition in a manner that echoes Rolle's own approach to sensual experience. Cunningham writes that Scotus proposes two modes of cognition:

> for abstract cognition this object is the species which is similar to the extramental object that is itself the cause of intuitive cognition. The latter type of cognition is rather conditional upon the presence and existence of the object (*praesentialier existens*). It is this prerequisite which enables Scotus to introduce a further distinction, namely that of perfect and imperfect intuitive cognition. Perfect intuitive cognition is the aforementioned cognition of a present and existing object, and imperfect intuitive cognition is a cognition that involves intuition of objects that were once present and existing, but are no longer so.[13]

Imperfect intuitive cognition is what leads to memory. The interworking of these various kinds of cognition is fundamental to Rolle's comprehension of divine phenomena. At the same time, Rolle's phenomenology emphasizes a sensuousness of non-revelation—the surfaces of God do not give up complete stories as a way to reflect the mystery of the divine.[14] In effect, Rolle is creating a theology of surface *and* depth: the fire, sweetness, and song can be felt, but the varieties of experience and meaning in these three phenomena are inexhaustible. Thus, the *Incendium Amoris* (and the works of Rolle *writ large*) prove frustrating, easily dismissed by critics, and problematic in its theological systematics because of its attempts (and failures) to render a totalizing theological and philosophical system. Queer theology helps in thinking about open-ended theologies such as Rolle's, as his works disrupt normative being and push divine communication into new configurations.

For Sara Ahmed, phenomenology is a way to register significance. She writes that "phenomenology can offer a resource for queer studies insofar as it emphasizes the importance of lived experience, the intentionality of consciousness, the significance of nearness or what is ready-to-hand, and the role of repeated and habitual actions in shaping bodies and worlds."[15] As we proceed, I want to use Ahmed's rubric: how does Rolle render lived experience; how does he represent significance? The question of Rolle's rendering of significance is important in that one of the criticisms of Rolle is that his work does not present any kind of organized message. But, this need for systematization ignores the role of intentionality and the shaping of the body in queer ways as Ahmed heralds.

Malcolm Moyes' introduction to Rolle's *Expositio Super Novem Lectiones* illustrates this criticism of Rolle as unsystematic. Moyes writes that Rolle's work

> is both strengthened and debilitated by the Bernardine writings Rolle drew upon and the way he drew upon them: it is his strength because the sensuous and highly-charged Bernardine ideas and expressions, detached from their original context, either by Rolle or the intermediate Bernardine texts that he utilized, did not commit his spirituality to a strict theoretical framework, allowing the larger suggestive power of his rhetoric to flow unobstructed; it is his weakness because the dislocation noted above and the consequent impression of Rolle's failure to analyze and relate the complexities of what must precede the apparently esoteric experiences that he seeks to describe in terms of "calor," "canor," and "dulcor," necessarily brings into question both the nature of those experiences and therefore his competence as a teacher and director of souls.[16]

Moyes points out both that Rolle lacks a theological framework which is a strength allowing Rolle to have "suggestive power" in his work, but, despite this apparent "strength," it is also a weakness by wresting Bernardine imagery from its context allegedly preventing Rolle from analyzing his experience.[17] Despite Moyes excellent analysis elsewhere in his introduction, I hope to show Moyes incorrect in terms of a "theological framework" in this chapter since Rolle's queer, theological framework, albeit not "standard" or scholastic by any stretch of the imagination is an attempt to reflect the difficulty of contemplation, the openness of queer embodiment, and the frustrations inherent in illustrating the *nubility* of divinity.[18] Rolle advocates a shaping of the body that experiences the divine through a use of the senses that does not conform to traditional body boundaries, one of his most repeated, yet queer, ideas. The eremitic body is not a body in the traditional sense; it is a body of flows of fire, sweetness, and song. Thus, Rolle's theology as it is connected to his phenomenology is *queer* as it resists normalizing boundaries in terms of body, touch, and love, and is very much concerned with orienting the body Godward in non-normative ways.

Rolle's discussion of the preparation of the body that I will discuss below addresses the problem of subjectivity in that the *author* of traditional T-theology stands as authority. Rolle casts his authorial body as one of passivity, reception, and humility (within the Pride event). The body is opened and God is recovered within it—the passive body comes to understand its own fullness. Rolle writes of the appearing object and the withdrawing object that is God. At the same time, Rolle reorients language toward the mystery of phenomenon that *resists* a full systematization.[19] In relating such things as the fire, sweetness, and song of Love, Rolle presents the phenomenological reduction: "a 'transcending passage' from the world to what is absolute, to what is, in other words, non-relative or non-human."[20] Rolle does have "suggestive power" in his work, and it is in this queer suggestive power—suggesting other ways to live, for example, or a new way to orient the body in terms of new uses of the senses—that we get his queer, open-ended mystical phenomenology.

What Rolle describes in the *Incendium Amoris* (and in other works I will deal with in this chapter such as *Ego Dormio* and *Desyre and Delit*) is a phenomenology of fire, sweetness, and song. This meditation on phenomenology is key for Rolle since in the act of recounting his own experience, and registering the frustration in wrapping language around this experience, he is *also* contemplating a phenomenology for God—how does God react, feel, and touch the contemplative? Conversely, how does this lead to the contemplative touching God? These touches, not necessarily with the skin, are forms of divine communication. Rolle's work plays with the gap between God's and the mystic's experience.[21]

The guiding principle in this chapter is setting in dialogue Rolle's phenomenology with various forms of twentieth and twenty-first century phenomenology. As a shorthand, I am going to use Heidegger's definition of phenomenology to interrogate Rolle's mystical experience. Heidegger writes:

> What is phenomenology? What is phenomenon? Here this can be itself indicated only formally. Each experience—as experi*encing*, and what is experi*enced*—can "be taken in the phenomenon" that is to say, one can ask:
>
> 1. After the original "*what*," that is experience therein (*content*).
> 2. After the original "*how*," in which it is experience (relation).
> 3. After the original "*how*," in which the relational meaning is *enacted* (*enactment*).
>
> But these three directions of sense (content-, relational-, enactment-sense) do not simply coexist. "Phenomenon" is the totality of the sense in these three directions.[22]

In this Heideggarian manner, we are also pursuing Rolle in three directions. We are attempting to take account of what he experienced, to explore how Rolle experienced it, and, finally, to see how Rolle relates the enacting of the phenomenon. This third direction is important in accounting for queer phenomenon as it is this direction that keeps the phenomenon "open" and in direct opposition to a purely scientific account: "there is no insertion into a material domain, but rather the opposite: the formal indication is a defense, a preliminary *securing*, so that the enactment-character remains free."[23] The "free" enactment character dovetails with this gap of mystical theology as an open and queer way of religious practice. As much as we account for Rolle's phenomenology, he also leaves the experience open. For example, and as I will discuss below in more detail, Rolle writes that in his triumvirate of sweetness, song, and fire, although he experienced sweetness first and it lead to fire and song, any one of these phenomenon can lead to the others. They overlap; they are not bounded experiences. This free enactment-character finds realization in the describing of the phenomenon. Rolle is experiencing *either* God or love of God, but the *content* of God's Being is left hazy. With Rolle, then, the reader or the hermit may meditate on the question, *What is this God that touches me?*

The Fire-Heart

There are a number of different objects that form an eremitic-assemblage in this chapter: fire, song, hermits, prayer, the body, God. In entering in a relationship with each object, the body encounters phenomena. As Adam S. Miller writes, the stuff of the world including prayer and the other stuff of religion constitute a world and "these objects traverse me, enable me, compose me. They bind me and resist me and they make the world available to me."[24] For example, the hermit *burns* with fire in his heart. The contemplative body *sits* in contemplation. God *dwells* in the heart. Feeling fire, sitting, dwelling: these are all phenomenon. How do we account for them? How do they have significance? Object-oriented philosophers and theologians such as Graham Harman and Adam Miller assist me in thinking about the phenomenon of objects in metaphorical and theological contexts.

Graham Harman writes that "the key to phenomenology is the notion of intentionality: the well-known axiom that consciousness is always conscious of something."[25] In Rolle's case intentionality is the opening oneself to God (as Creator, as an aspect of the whole Triune God) and He is present in terms of his effects on the contemplative's body.[26] Mystical theology wrestles with this problem at the level of language; Julian of Norwich's visions and her thirty-year meditation on their meaning illustrate the problem of rendering *seeing* into *meaning*.[27] Mystical phenomenon may be present, but for the mystic, the cause of that phenomenon—the object itself, God, angel, event, tableaux—are incapable of being captured in language completely. The object, as Sara Ahmed and Harman indicate does not present all of its sides to the senses. We could call mystical experience a "concrete experience"[28] and link it to traditional phenomenology, but it is a queer phenomenology, too, as Sara Ahmed would frame it, in that the "conditions of emergence,"[29] the thing-in-itself—in this case, God—is not a stable thing.

The striving toward stability and struggle of instability is a hallmark of a Rollean mystical theology. Richard Rolle begins *Incendium Amoris* with a note of incredulity: "I cannot begin to tell you how surprised I was the first time I felt my heart begin to warm."[30] Rolle is unable to decide on the *reality* of this feeling, and, in fact, he spends the majority of the "Prologue" to the *Incendium* meditating on the very instability of his self in the mystical phenomenon in a mode of what Karma Lochrie calls "abjection." Abjection is an

> ordeal of the self in which "nothing is familiar." [...] Abjection is the result of the Fall, whence the boundaries of the body and soul were violated. Because the flesh is heterogeneous—neither body nor soul, but carnal and spiritual at the same time—abjection poses a continual threat to the Christian subject. Yet it also offers a radical notion of perfection. The excess of drives—those heaving powers of the flesh—topples over into love of God.[31]

As we will see, Rolle proposes such a notion of excess and perfection in his prescription for contemplative success. And, in his prologue, we also get a sense of Rolle's abjection. The warmth in his heart is not familiar and flows over. How to account for this overflowing? Rolle's strategy, then, is to account for the body's permeability. Rolle's self-distancing in his account places him as observer to his own experience. On the one hand, he is attempting a first-hand narrative; on the other hand, he wants to know what it means—its significance. He cannot totally remove himself from the phenomena. Rolle analyzes himself—knows himself—by utilizing the experience of divine warmth, a *surprising* experience, by attempting to narrativize and order it. Rolle validates the experience by rendering it into a process.

Rolle asserts that "it was real warmth, too [...] and felt as if it were actually on fire."[32] Even in this sentence Rolle begins to contemplate the space between certainty and understanding divine mystery—"as if" [or "quasi" in the original Latin][33]—as Rolle elides his experience so that by the end of the paragraph he writes, "it set my soul aglow as if a real fire was burning there."[34] The fire is ready-to-hand, as Conor Cunningham points out, as the ready-to-hand is "a phenomenon [that] entails a withdrawal. In this sense one cannot settle the matter, there can be no presumption, as that which *is*, is only as it withdraws."[35] Rolle's "quasi" deserves contemplation because it signals the withdrawal of the phenomena. This is not a fire in terms of burning wood, for example. Rolle puts forward the power of metaphoric language and its capabilities. In employing the "quasi," Rolle stops an immediate narrative and contemplative univocity[36] in order to emphasize that his fire-heart contains an overflowing of meaning. This fire-heart is better than any fire one could experience. But, he also immediately enters into the realm of figurative language (analogy) as a signal that we have left the mortal and normative to think through the divine and queer.

Harman's work on metaphor in his *Guerilla Metaphysics* helps in thinking through the problem of fire that Rolle puts forth here. Harman's object-oriented ontology (OOO) posits that objects are the central problem of philosophy. OOO also displaces the human in thinking through ontology and phenomenology. As Harman writes, "the real weakness of phenomenology is its failure to capture the objecthood of objects, the 'I' of sailboats and moons, by granting them an intimate interior of their own."[37] Harman puts forth that metaphor (and jokes) take the steps to do just this: "the fate of language, as of perception and [. . .] of all relation, is forever to translate the dark and inward into the tangible and outward, a task at which it is always comes up short given the infinite depth of things."[38] Language, as I have been insisting, is one of the problems of mystical writing because it places metaphorical language in the forefront and, thus, mystical *meaning* and relations are infinite. The appeal of metaphors is that they work as a bridge for the phenomenology of the mystical event.[39] For Harman (borrowing from Ortega), metaphors provide us with a link between things that are *inessential*. In comparing a cypress tree to a flame, for example, the connection is not between something that they share; rather, it is the inessential qualities (in this case, the shape) that prove the aesthetic satisfaction in the metaphor. For Harman, "the cypress is not only an image sparkling with diverse features, but also a murky underground unity *for me*, and not just in its inner executant self. And it is from this strange concealed integrity of individual images that metaphor draws its power—not from the genuine reality of each thing, which language is powerless to unveil."[40] Harman further points out that metaphor encourages us to experience *with* this new thing, "a new object born in our midst in the very moment it is named."[41]

I want to slow down and think through Rolle's new fire-heart as matter and as metaphor. He has experienced a fire in his heart, a warmth-like fire. His heart "felt like it was actually on fire."[42] The connection between warmth and the heart is not a stretch, actually. Blood is warm. Yet, Rolle wants to reveal a dimension of the heart that is both familiar *and* strange. We only have a sense of the heart as warm from the blood that flows through it, and even then only when the blood exits the skin. We do not experience the heart as hot (just as we do not experience our liver or spleen as hot), as burning, as it beats inside our chest. In thinking of things like "heartburn," we know that our heart is actually not afflicted, rather it is the acid reflux in our esophagus and a resultant effect in the nerves that leads to that feeling—the experience of heartburn is anatomically in front of our heart. So, our everyday experience of the heart is not that of *burning*. The heart then, in Rolle's experience, is a feeling that supersedes and overflows the everyday experience of the heart. The heart here is hot. In connecting the heart with a heat, Rolle puts the heart in the center of his experience; as well, he reorients the heart—gestures toward how we do not know our own heart in that we do not usually experience the heart as heat and shows that we take the heart for granted. It beats in our chest, and we usually do not take notice of it unless it falls outside the beat. What happens when it feels like it is on fire? How disorienting would it be to feel a burning heart? The touch of the divine renders the heart queer. This exposition in thinking through the heart/fire metaphor underlies thinking about Rolle's discussion of the body, indwelling, and God's presence. This metaphor opens up contemplative phenomenon in thinking about the body *differently*. The senses we use to know and understand the heart are reoriented inwardly, Godwardly; the contemplative becomes aware of the heart's capabilities.

By the end of the prologue to the *Incendium Amoris*, Rolle is calling the fire a metaphor (flammam quam sub metaphora ignem appellaui, eo quod urit et lucet)[43] but what makes it metaphorical is the power of awakened consciousness that it creates: he calls it "flammam" "because it burns and enlightens"[44] The heart and the fire are intertwined in their causality. The heart is enlightening and burning as it has become a heart of fire. The metaphor reveals *inessential* qualities—and I think Harman does not mean inessential as in "unimportant" rather, going along with his later discussion about the depths of objects, he is suggesting that these are qualities that are hidden from us. In this case, then, the heart of fire is hidden from Rolle in its entirety but is partly realized with a divine touch.

The disruption of clear causal links is the delight of Rolle's attempt to live within these inessential aesthetic touches of metaphor. In other words, in thinking through the heat/fire, the link between spark and wood is short-circuited. Rolle connects this gift with the Creator, but the source of the heat—as we see a lit candle and feel the warmth it puts off and know it was the flame of the candle providing the heat of the candle by placing our hand near it—is never *seen* by Rolle or by his readers. For Rolle the cause of these things—sweetness, song, or heat—is Non-Being, one that does not need to appear, one that only shows its surfaces in order to provide a reaction in embodiment. The ontology of the heart's realness in God is revealed through this embodied reaction: Rolle's ontology and phenomenology is most evident as it is expressed in these queer relations.

What normally causes a fire is eschewed for the inner quality of the heart. Rolle only suggests that his heart is on fire, but he leaves out a definitive causal link other than "the gift of my Maker."[45] Rolle renders phenomenon into metaphor and in the meantime opens up the gap between what causes the fire and what constitutes the fire. Perhaps in metaphor, Rolle contemplates the *beyond*; in other words, Rolle dissolves the divide between literalness and metaphoric language.

Rolle contrasts his holy heat with situations in which he experiences cold. When Rolle is too relaxed or too tired or too "absorbed in worldly interests," he feels cold.[46] This physical fatigue will be addressed later when Rolle meditates on physical position and how he should be positioned to meditate; however, for now, I will note that this cold subsides when he becomes focused and "stands in [his] Saviour's presence."[47] The cold, much like the heat, is processed through Rolle's body—when his body and mind are fatigued or distracted, Rolle loses the heat. It is a mystical state, as well. The mystic's goal, then, is to be warm. Warmth, however, is elusive as Rolle will point out again and again, because of a preponderance of cold. Thus, the eremitic body must think through this cold deception to strive for a permanent warmth.

Rolle challenges his reader with a difficult task: first, one must attend to a real phenomenon that is metaphor, a metaphor that contains a sensation that Rolle insists he felt. Next, the reader steps out of the normative use of language, literalness, and live within the surprise that is found in the conjunctions of metaphors. This queer form of living increases the possibilities of the senses; living within figurative language presents phenomena in new configurations. Rolle puts forth other demands, too. In the *Incendium Amoris*, Rolle insists that we read the experience metaphorically while preparing the reader to experience these same experiences. Rolle insists, further, that his text is for the "simple and unlearned," yet his strategy is to utilize complicated Biblical exegesis of Jonah and Jeremiah and create a system of enlightenment based on older theology found in Richard of St. Victor, Bernard, and Augustine.

As Heidegger asks, "What does relation to God mean? Meaningfully and constitutedly, only to be formulated as a comportment of consciousness, not for instance, ontically, as being next to, or 'under' as (absolute) being. Rather the opposite holds: our experiential comportment to God—the primary one, because welling up within us by grace—gives direction to the specially *religious* constitution of 'God' as a phenomenological object."[48] Along with Heidegger, I am positing that Rolle's mystical phenomenology is a consideration of fire, sweetness, and song as the touch of objects within a new *capability* for a queer, eremitic body.

The Experience of God's Touch: Sweetness

The surprise of eremitic-becoming is found in the overflowing sweetness that challenges the senses. Rolle presents us with mystical phenomenon—fire, sweetness, song—in a frame that works at queering the hermit-contemplative. These phenomena are a major part of Rolle's major texts—*Incendium Amoris* and *The Form of Living*. While *Incendium Amoris* can be read as a defense of the eremitic life—a life in which Rolle is embarking—*The Form of Living* is written for Margaret Kirkby at the end of his life. Rolle presents that text as a rule for contemplative and anchoritic living. As discussed in Chapter 2, both works, contemplate the anxiety of defining the contours of the hermit. In other words, Rolle is very much concerned with being able to propose eremitic being as a queer response to the normative Christianity surrounding him and define the process as coming out of adversity with those normalizing sins and hypocrites. His solution to this anxiety is to emphasize the phenomenology of the hermit—the experience of contemplative living that will zero in on a contemplative experience and reify the contemplative ego. Rolle is not necessarily always successful in explanation because of the very hiddenness of God within the eremitic body.

What is perhaps most interesting in Rolle's pursuit of mystical experience is the trusting of this withdrawing source of phenomena. Duns Scotus proposes this metaphor for the understanding of God:

> the following example is used to explain how God can be the reason why we know and yet not be known in Himself. Some sunlight is reflected while other rays come directly from the source. And even though the sun is the reason why we see something by reflected sunlight the sun is not seen. But for an object illumined by direct light, the sun is a reason for knowing that is also known. In similar fashion, then, when the Uncreated Light as it were illumines an intellect by a direct glance, then this Light as seen is the reason for seeing the other things in it. In the present life, however, this Uncreated

> Light illumines our intellect indirectly as it were. Consequently, though unseen itself, it is the reason why our intellect sees.[49]

Faith provides the mystic with the ground of experience who do not need a clear physical touch of a physical God to experience the presence of God. The touch causes physical perturbations. They do not need to be a Thomas poking their hand into the wound of the resurrected Christ. Instead, as Scotus explores, Rolle opens his body to the experience and this open body must deal with the capability of the fire-heart and the uncertainty of causality.

God's touch is experienced in plural, or as Rolle would remark, His presence only will *be* what the contemplative is capable of receiving. Cunningham writes

> it is the *strangeness* of phenomena that is the ontological clue which intimates the possibility of restating the desired question. Phenomena arrive within a world which perpetually reenacts their arrival. Thus every entity is disclosed within Dasein's concernful dealings, as that which *shows* itself in *withdrawing*; this is the excess of presence [...].[50]

God is revealed in degrees and, therefore, is always in excess. With Rolle we could consider that God could not always be known in the experience of fire, sweetness, or song—maybe it would be silence or cold or water—it would only reflect what the hermit-contemplative was oriented to experiencing. Thus the hermit-contemplative expresses a queer way of being in the world as they are always experiencing the divine touch differently.

How do body and God touch? In his epistle, *Desyre and Delit*, Rolle writes that when a man "felis hym in þat degree, than es a man circumsysede gastely when all oþer besynes and affeccyons and thoghtes are drawen away owte of his saule, that he may hafe ryste in Goddes lufe, withowtten tagillynge of oþer thynges. The delyte es wondirfull: it is se heghe, þat na thoghte may reche þarto to bring it doun."[51] The turning to God results in a spiritual circumcision—something is cut away, "drawnen owte"—and much like the physical foreskin, reduced to the trace of memory. The foreskin is linked to thoughts about earthly things and by cutting it away the contemplative lives with the palimpsest of the mark of the world and the Real of the divine—the (spiritual) penis transformed into something new. However, much like the fire, the spiritual circumcision is a kind of touch. It is significant that Rolle focuses on the penis and its excised foreskin as a way to configure desire. Spiritual circumcision is a relational sign of the mark of the earth on the skin—the body once had this fleshly spiritual excess, but now it is removed transforming desire. This spiritual foreskin becomes a reminder of how the contemplative continues their process toward the divine through the divine touch on their spiritual member.

Notice, as well, "delyte" (which is a stand-in for Rolle's *dulcor* or sweetness in his other works) allows the soul to go higher—though it cannot completely attain its goal without God. Rolle cuts a line between thinking and a "delyte" which goes beyond thinking. Delight or sweetness is a mental state characterized by the loss of self found in immersion. Rolle also draws this distinction in the *Incendium Amoris*.[52] Rolle writes, quoting Corinthians, that "knowledge without love does not edify or contribute to our eternal salvation, it merely puffs up our own dreadful loss."[53] Later, Rolle writes that true understanding will lead one to God.[54] They close in on one another in these objects of fire, sweetness, and song.[55]

This contemplation of immersive *dulcor* is repeated in Rolle's epistle, *Ego Dormio*, the title and first line taken from *Song of Songs* 5:2: "ego dormio et cor meum vigilat." In this epistle, Rolle sets up the body's position vis-a-vis a God event. The self sleeps, the ego, but the heart remains alert (it is Foucault's and Edelman's formulation of the self split from the self); they are separate capabilities. Rolle emphasizes repose here; in this epistle, Rolle represents God's love as ever-present, it is up to the addressee of this epistle to prepare themselves for Him. Rolle writes, "I wil becum a messager to brynge þe to his bed þat hath mad þe and boght þe, Crist, þe kynges son of heuyn, for he wil wed þe if þou wil loue hym."[56] God in this situation is the bed-maker, the lover who is willing, but not necessarily triumphant in love, or sure of himself, as Rolle remarks. In the erotic economy of this epistle, Christ will wed, this marriage will be consummated, if the addressee will open themselves to love Him. The decision to love God, despite the heart's openness to God's love, is evident in the formula: my body sleeps, but my heart is vigilant. The vigilant heart is the focus, the reposed body allows the heart to work—it is within the heart that the decision will be made, the "vigilat" heart works on God.

The goal in *Ego Dormio* is to join the opened-self with God. As Rolle warns, "for whils þi hert is holdynge to loue of any bodily thynge, þou may not perfitly be cowpled with God."[57] The language of coupling indicates an erotic colocality based in un-mappable desire. The hermit will realize the body's hidden eroto-spiritual capability so that the contemplative can couple with

God. Rolle offers a sense of what he means by sweetness when he writes that: "men thynke it swet to syn, bot har hire þat is ordeyned for ham is bitterer þan galle, sowrer þan attyre, wors þan al þe woo þat men can þynke in erth."[58] This is not the sweetness found in contemplation; rather, this is misleading sweetness, a sweetness that leads to death. The first degree of contemplation that Rolle describes in the *Ego Dormio* is reorienting oneself to Law, the second degree of contemplation, then, leads one to study oneself and

> forsake al þe world and þi fadyre and þi modyre and al þi kyn, and follow Crist in pouert. In þis degree þou shalt study how clene þou may be in herte, and how chaste in body, and gyf þe to mekenesse, suffrynge, and buxumnesse. And loke how faire þou may make þi soule in vertuʒ and hate al vices, so þat þi lif be gostly.[59]

The goal in this stage is to transform the life of the contemplative from one of worldly concerns to one directed toward the spiritual. The phrase "þi life be gostly" is worth extra consideration as there are two levels of life existing at the same time. Much like his burning heart, Rolle is pointing out that we are not originally directed toward the spiritual. Ontologically it is already there; the contemplative needs to notice it. In noticing the divine while in practice of contemplation, the contemplatives' life becomes something else; "swetter þan any erthly þynge."[60]

Within this phenomenon of immersive sweetness, the contemplative will feel the burning of fire in their heart. At this level, the contemplative will be filled with the Holy Ghost and no longer worry about earthly things. It is when all earthly things are put away that the contemplative will feel: "[þ]e lust st[e]l bi þi o to þynke of Crist, and to be in mych praynge, for þrogh good þoghtes and holy praiers þi hert shal be mad brennynge in þe loue of Ihesu Crist and þan shal þou fele swetnesse annd gostlu ioy, both in praynge and þynkynge".[61] Lust is reoriented here, not to fleshly things, but the desire of Christ. Rolle is suggesting a reorientation here—lust (much like the discussion of pride in Chapter 1) is not sinful if it is inspired by the divine touch. The hermit must use lust to draw closer to God.

If the hermit intends to succeed in these initial levels of the contemplative life, the third is not in their power to fulfill. God "cheseth whom he wil to do þat here is saird, or other thynge in oþer maner, as he gifeth men grace har hele."[62] However, "who-so is in þis degree, wisdome, he hath and discrecioun, to lyve at Goddis wille."[63] It is in this level that the "goostly egh" is taken up and illuminated.[64] Then, Rolle writes, one will feel the burning in the heart, the fullness of immersive sweetness, and, finally, all "þi praiers turneth in to ioyful songe and þi þoghtes to melodi. Þan Ihesu is all þi desire, al þi delit, al þi ioy, al þi solace, al þi comforte, so þat on hym wil euer be þi songe, and [in] hym al þi rest. Þan may þou say 'I slepe and my hert waketh'."[65] As Rolle announces toward the end of *Ego Dormio*, "þe fyre of loue hath brent away al þe roust of syn."[66] The body has rusted in its earthly cares, but the fire of love has burnt away the rust, revealing the refigured, reborn body underneath.

Rolle ends *Ego Dormio* with a lyric that brings back the theme of coupling as desire for God:

> When wil þou rewe on me, Ihesu, þat I myght with þe be,
> To loue and loke on þe? My sete ordayn for me,
> And set þou me þerin, for þan [may] we neuer twyn,
> And I þi loue shal synge þrogh syght in þy shynynge
> In heuyn withouten endynge.[67]

Rolle here reinforces the power in being seated. As he is seated in contemplation, he shall be seated in heaven for eternity. And God will seat him there. He is orienting his body to that of the divine through his seated repose. Here is an example of passive immanence.[68] Rolle has no power in his subjectivity at this point in that he will be able to look, love, and sing with God. In this sitting, they will never be uncoupled. Rolle finishes the lyric with a combination of phenomena—a phenomenology of heaven— where he will sing by looking. As his eyes are locked on God (and God on his eyes), then Rolle will sing with light. The body has hidden depths that are activated when the divine object touches it in various ways.[69] The eyes can sing. The song is rendered visible as light. Although in erotic coupling there is a decoupling, here there will not be a release, a leaving. God and Rolle (or God and the hermit-contemplative) will be coupled through eternity in an ecstatic sweetness.

The Phenomenon of Embodied Language: Sitting in the Direction of God

Rolle is remapping the body when he describes the fire-heart and immersive sweetness. Adam Kotsko argues that we need to think about the human differently: "humanity stands at a nodal point in the universe, at a nexus of rich variety of relationships. This is true at the level of the individual, as the patristic authors attempted to indicate by their rejections of a monadic soul and their insistence that the human being is the relationship between body and soul—that is, even the individual is relational 'all the way down'."[70] In the case of *Ego Dormio*, the eremitic body emerges from the sweetness that characterizes the relationship between God and hermit. Rolle encourages the addressee to take the next step of contemplative life—to understand the relational possibilities of their body and God's presence there.

Rolle propose a sensual rhetoric in his work, one, according to Gordon Rudy, that is characterized by "somatic language—that […] refers to the human body. […] the sensory language that theologians use to talk about relations between people and God is patterned on and refers to relations between bodies; that is relations between the embodied self and other persons and things."[71] Sensual language is a reflection of the relationship between people and God; Kotsko, emphasizing the work a body does as a reflection of the fidelity to Christ and its relational nature, and Rudy, who argues for sensual language as between bodies, highlights this power of the phenomenon of language to create relations between the body, soul, and God. Language is relational with embodiment; much like language can be experimented with, extended, bent, so too can the body.

When Rolle writes that he feels a fire in his heart—it is a link between his heart and the love of God. As well, God is touching that heart, and the body has been reshaped to center on and see and feel *through* the heart. The heart is the seat that God takes. Rudy continues in a similar vein as Kotsko: "we know God not insofar as we are spirit but as whole human persons, as selves who are both body and soul. They [mystics] assume that we are able to know and be with him because we are both spirit and matter, as Christ was."[72] This relationship is expressed in the phenomena of language, through *canor* for example (which I will focus on in Chapter 4). Rolle explores this "between" of body and soul through his use of fire, sweetness, and song.[73]

In many of his texts, Rolle proposes degrees of love for the addressee to follow as a way to explore the "between" of God and lover. There are sensual ways to prepare the body for loving God. Although the aim is to direct the body to sleep and the heart to rise higher—we can think of the opening psalm in *Ego Dormio* as a commentary on the disconnect of the body and heart—the body must be opened to the already "vigilat" heart. As discussed in Chapter 2, the first level is to hold true to the Ten Commandments, keeping away from the deadly sins, and to become

3 THE PHENOMENOLOGY OF THE OPEN BODY 73

"stabil in þe trouth of holy chirch."[74] The second degree of love is to forsake the world: "þi fadyre and þi modyre and al þi kyn, and follow Crist in pouerte."[75] Holding the commandments is to align oneself to Church life, to hold oneself to the Law, to give up world gifts is to show what Law One has chosen, that of the world (respect for family connections) or Christ (the dissolution of those connections).[76] Finally, Rolle writes that the final degree of love is the contemplative life. Rolle writes that not everyone rises to this kind of living; it is up to God to reach out.[77]

Part of Rolle's textual praxis is to reflect the struggle of waiting as a problem of stability. Rolle's movement from place to place because of his critiques of normative living is no secret—he references them in the *Incendium*—but the reasons for his actions are often queer. The queer nature of the hermit, as related by Rolle, is reflected in his own circuitous route in becoming a hermit: he himself was never a *sanctioned* hermit. Rolle challenges the idea that one can must an eremitic life with an official stamp or norm. Rolle struggles with this problem of normative spirituality: the hermit flirts with the gap between the abnormal (heretic) and the normal (the enclosed religious, the monk) without landing in any clear place. Rolle's spiritual queerness is recognized in the ways that his work was adopted by other marginalized groups, such as the Lollards, after his death.[78]

In order to examine that creation of the eremitic body as a seated body, let us go back to that initial mystical moment in the *Incendium Amoris*. Rolle describes his experience as

> sitting in a certain chapel, delighting in the sweetness of prayer or meditation when suddenly I felt within myself an unusually pleasant heat. At first I wondered where it came from, but it was not long before I realized that it was from none of God's creatures, but from the Creator himself [...]. But it was just over nine months before a conscious and incredibly sweet warmth kindled me, and I knew the infusion and understanding of heavenly, spiritual sounds, sounds which pertain to the song of eternal praise, and to the sweetness of unheard melody: sounds which cannot be known of heard save by him who has received it, and who must himself be clean and separate from the things of the earth.[79]

Rolle has prepared us for the fruits that come with sitting in meditation. The Creator awakens Rolle's capabilities. The heat results from immersive sweetness. Thus, Rolle is *already* experiencing sweetness at this moment, or experiencing sweetness alongside fire—he has prepared his body in his seated repose for a divine communication—though he did not know that the phenomenon of fire would be the experience of God.[80]

Rolle's work on turning himself to God follows the contours of Sara Ahmed's discussion of orientation. Ahmed asks: "what does it mean for sexuality to be lived as orientated? What difference does it make 'what' or 'who' we are orientated towards in the very directions of our desire? If orientation is a matter of how we reside in space, then sexual orientation might also be a matter of residence."[81] Although Ahmed is emphasizing sexual orientation, it is worth extrapolating her questions to the case of Rolle since he is orientating himself to an object of desire that is marked by a queer, spiritual eroticism not circumscribed by hetero-normative codes. Ahmed's phenomenological questions ring true for Rolle, as well, in that we can ask what happens when he is orientated toward God? What does he open himself to? How does his embodied residence affect the experience?

As Rolle reshapes his body, and with that shaping orients his desire Godward, his experiences become more and more attuned to the divine. As Ahmed writes, "bodies do not dwell in spaces that are exterior but rather are shaped by their dwellings and take shape by dwelling."[82] Rolle's insistence on sitting, on providing a place of stability for God, are important—he is preparing his body for a revelation of indwelling and must orient his body in a certain direction. Rolle writes, that the contemplative, busy with love, "consistently practices righteousness until such time as he led up to his God, to sit with the heaven-born on an everlasting throne."[83] His body must be made welcoming to the divine as it echoes divine sitting. Placing the body in a sitting position immediately places that body outside of normative, physical activity as well as normative time. The need to move, to work, to stand, to walk—these actions are irrelevant to Rolle's contemplation and, thus, his phenomenology derives from the position of a sitting body. The body sits and is made into a shape, we may call it a cushion, a comfortable lap. In sitting, the body becomes chair-like, something one can take comfort in. In this kind of repose, Rolle's body is open to God's dwelling and mimics the divine throne. Rolle embodies queer temporalities; it becomes a link between mortal and divine worlds.

The fire, song, and sweetness are surprising, and Rolle wrestles with the shock of phenomena. As Ahmed comments regarding the work of Husserl: "phenomenology for Husserl means apprehending the object as if it were unfamiliar, so that we can attend to the flow of perception itself."[84] Rolle's ontology and phenomenology attends to this flowing perception. He is democratic in his wish for everyone to burn with the fire of love: "and so because I would stir up by the means *every man* to love God, and because I am trying to make plain the ardent nature of love and how it is supernatural, the title selected for this book will be the *Incendium*."[85] Unlike the *Cloud*-author who spends many paragraphs on who should not read his book, Rolle is hoping that all will attend to their bodies, orient themselves to God, sit, and experience the fire. As Lawlor writes, "the powerlessness of the experience gives me power to think otherwise and to become new."[86] This newness is connected with experiencing the body itself differently. As Rolle admits, the fire will burn differently depending on "our particular capacity"; however, everyone is able to *become hermit*.

Rolle's appeal to the reception of phenomena within a seated, spatiality configured within the hermit indicates queer orientation and *direction*. Rolle writes that the soul must be pointed "Godward": "Godward is where the elect have their thoughts directed."[87] The elect only deal with "mundane" matters when necessary. Rolle is able to draw the line between an attitude-toward-the-world and that which is directed-toward-God. Immersion in the divine phenomenon erases the separation of worlds. As Rolle turns himself Godward, the more his body and soul are reoriented, the line between God and world is eased. Rolle has no need for the concerns of the world, in terms of "everydayness," rather as his contemplative life is directed toward God, his relationship with the world is changed so that matters of simple living are not necessarily matters of concern as matters of rote.

One cannot have mystical experience without the phenomenon of the stability of mind: "when they have attained the gravity of behavior so necessary and have achieved a certain stability of mind [. . .] it is then they can feel some joy in loving God."[88] Rolle's formula is noteworthy: only in the stability of mind, a *Godwardness,* when the contemplative has mastered an orientation, only then will they be able to experience divine communication. Rolle appeals to a certain seriousness, *gravitas,* to the spiritual life, but it is the stability that cleans the weeds of worldly matters. Stability is the antidote to distractions, the neutralizer for the enticement of worldly matters.

The stability of mind (as a way to void the world from the soul so God can take up residence) manifests itself in the act of sitting down. For Rolle, the phenomena of sitting and stability are intertwined. Rolle takes from Jeremiah the significance of sitting: "*it is good for a man to bear the yoke of the Lord in his youth. He will sit in solitude and quiet and will raise himself up.*"[89] This sitting and quiet in solitude matches the hermit's queer-orientation to the world: "all the while he is indifferent to worldly power love indwells the heart of the solitary."[90] The normative world is left behind for the overflowing Love within.

Thus, Rolle lines up three parallel threads of contemplative experience: pointing the self-Godward, sitting, and, becoming immersed by indwelling love. Stability is the central phenomenon brought on by sitting, though not in any specific *place* necessarily. Rolle writes that to love God involves heat, song, and sweetness, but these can only be experienced when he is sitting:

> If I were to stand up when I was engaged in contemplation or to walk about or even to live prostrate on the ground, I found that I failed to attain those three and even seemed to be left in dryness. Consequently, if I were to hold on to and retain deep devotion I must sit.[91]

Sitting for Rolle is a way to keep the body open to God. As he explains walking about or standing turns the body and, thus, the soul toward the world. Rolle appeals to Aristotle: "it is the quiet sitting that makes the soul wise."[92] The sitting soul is quiet, stable. Rolle connects sitting to the "heights of contemplation."[93] The ability to be in a humble, physical position allows the contemplative to reach greater spiritual heights.

By Rolle's own admission, he had difficulty in finding physical places to be a hermit. This is perhaps why he spends so much time on the act of sitting and its subsequent phenomenon; it does not matter where one sits and practices stability: "I continually sought quiet, and that although I went from one place to another."[94] Rolle draws a line here between space and place, Godward and world. Space is stability, contemplation, taking up the space of sitting. Place, on the other hand, is the problem of the world. It is only in attention to space that the phenomenon of warmth, sweetness, and song occur.

These mystical phenomena are transforming to the opened body. While providing the stability and the focus, the body itself becomes a space for God. In preparing the space for God, then, the "lower" becomes more like God. The sweetness, song, and heat are aspects of God's being experienced by the queer, eremitic body. The lover experiences the love as transforming—they are no longer who they were and the borders of identity are erased in this unifying effect of love. For Rolle, the nature of love is "diffusive, unifying, and transforming."[95] Rolle emphasizes the soul's intentionality in his move "Godward." This movement Godward serves as a base for stability that further strengthens the soul's openness. Rolle describes this movement as "a giving up of everything that panders to vanity. It is afterwards that he is seized by the taste for eternal sweetness which is going to make him sing joyously for God."[96] For Rolle, the turning Godward is an assimilation: "every lover is assimilated to his beloved: love makes the loving one like what he loves."[97] This twinning of love moves the body and soul past its boundaries to join with God.

For Rolle, then, the stability of mind is key. Rolle recommends continual prayer as a way to achieve this state: "we ought always to be praying, or reading, or meditation and doing other useful things, so that our enemy never finds us idle."[98] The act of meditating, the act of prayers, keeps one focused on God. For Rolle not remaining focused leaves one cold. The absence of God (like the bottom of Hell in Dante's *Inferno*) leaves Rolle cold—a cold he can expiate only when he sits and allows the divine to work in him.

We come full circle. Cold does not leave a mark; it is absence. Unlike fire, unlike spiritual circumcision, there is no trace of God's touch in the cold. In many places in *Incendium Amoris*, Rolle writes that fire does something: "for the love to which we are rising by this work is hotter than any burning coal, and will undoubtedly leave its mark, because it will make our spirits glowing and splendid."[99] For Rolle fire's transformative properties leave us with something: "all is permeated with its [love of Christ] lovely pleasure, so that our inner nature seems to be turned into divine glory and a song of love."[100] These contemplative phenomena may not be fully understood, but they leave a trace and transform the body. God queers the hermit through a touch and the resultant phenomenal perturbations place the hermit permanently outside of normative life.

The opened body touches the divine in various ways. In living in metaphor, the power of fire and turning Godward in sweetness, Rolle has oriented the hermit's desire for God. God is touch and leaves a mark. As I will discuss in the next chapter, the song of love, *canor,* is a realization of the soul's mingling with the seated God, the fire-heart, and the immersive sweetness. In singing out, in turning Christ's seat into external song, into an event, a connection is forged between the phenomena of sweetness, heat, and song and the voice's expression of the Christ-name. Language and the breaking of language's limits externalize the internal, transformed soul. The lyric, as an expression of *canor*, focuses the name of Jesus on the creation of a space of contemplation, a divine ecology.

Notes

1. Conor Cunningham, *Genealogy of Nihilism* (New York: Routledge, 2002), p. 191.
2. Martin Heidegger, *The Phenomenology of Religious Life*. Translated by Matthias Fritsch and Jennifer Anna Gosetti-Ferencei (Bloomington: Indiana University Press, 2010), p. 86.
3. M.F. Wakelin, "Richard Rolle and the Language of Mystical Experience in the Fourteenth Century," *Downside Review* 97 (1979): p. 193.
4. Michael Warner, "Tongues Untied: Memoirs of a Pentecostal Boyhood" in *The Material Queer: A LesBiGay Cultural Studies Reader*. Ed. Donald Morton (Boulder, CO: Westview Press, 1996), p. 43.
5. Warner, "Tongues Untied," p. 43.
6. Eleanor Johnson, *Practicing Literary Theory in the Middle Ages* (Chicago: University of Chicago Press, 2013), p. 10.
7. Patrick S. Cheng, *Radical Love* (New York: Seabury Books, 2011), p. 139.
8. Annabelle Wilcox, "Phenomenology, Embodiment, and Political Efficacy" in *The Ashgate Research Companion to Queer Theory*. Ed. Noreen Giffney and Michael O'Rourke (Burlington, VT: Ashgate, 2010), pp. 96, 97.
9. Carolyn Dinshaw, *Getting Medieval: Sexualities and Communities, Pre- and Post-modern* (Durham: Duke, 1999), p. 12. As Leonard Lawlor also points out, "Hegel, of course, associates spirit with memory. Being memory, spirit allows for the inward feeling of unity with others that constitutes community," p. 218. *Derrida and Husserl: The Basic Problem of Phenomenology* (Bloomington: Indiana University Press, 2002).
10. Jean-Luc Nancy, *Being Singular Plural* (Standford: Standford University Press, 2000), p. 93.
11. For an exploration of the materialism that refutes the Manichean thinking surrounding body and soul inherent in discussions of the medieval body see Bill Burgwinkle, "Medieval Somatics." *The Cambridge Companion to the Body in Literature*. Ed. David Hillman and Ulrika Maude. (Cambridge: Cambridge University Press, 2015), pp. 10–23.
12. For connections between Scotus and Rolle see Ardis Butterfield, *The Familiar Enemy: Chaucer, Language, and Nation in the Hundred Years War* (Oxford: Oxford University Press, 2009) and Norman Tanner, *Ages of Faith: Popular Religion in Late Medieval England and Western Europe* (London: I.B. Tauris, 2009).
13. Conor Cunningham, p. 45. Also see John Duns Scotus "Parisian Proof for the Existence of God," in William A. Frank and Allan B. Wolter, *Duns Scotus Metaphysician,* (West Lafayette, IN: Purdue University Press, 1995), 40–107.

14. For a discussion of the interplay between body as text and text as body that informs my discussion, see Gail Weiss, "The Body as a Narrative Horizon," *Thinking the Limits of the Body*. Ed. Jeffrey Jerome Cohen and Gail Weiss (Albany: State University of New York Press, 2003), 25–38.
15. Sara Ahmed, *Queer Phenomenology* (Durham: Duke University Press, 2006), p. 2.
16. Malcolm Robert Moyes, "Richard Rolle's 'Expositio super Novem Lections Mortuorum: An Introduction" in Richard Rolle's *Expositio Super Novem Lectiones Mortuorum*, Volume I. (Salzburg: Institut für Anglistik und Amerikanistik, 1988), pp. 65–66.
17. Other critics also accuse Rolle of anti-intellectualism. For example, William F. Pollard writes that Rolle shares his anti-intellectualism with that of the *Cloud*-author. See William F. Pollard, "Richard Rolle and the 'Eye of the Heart'," p. 95. Probably the harshest (and possibly ad hominem) attack is by Louise Nelstrop in "The Merging of Eremitic and 'Affectivist' Spirituality in Richard Rolle's Reshaping of Contemplation" in *Viator: A Journal of Medieval and Renaissance Studies*, 35 (2004): 289–309. In that article, Nelstrop accuses Rolle of anti-intellectualism: "I hope to illustrate that Rolle also defines his understanding of contemplation in terms of a highly anti-intellectual understanding of 'affectivist' contemplation," p. 291. Later, Nelstrop writes, "Rolle emphasizes the essential nature of this internal enclosure linking it with the intellect. However, it is not an intellectual practice in any meaningful sense," p. 301. Moyes, Pollard, and Nelstrop use "anti-intellectualism," I think, as a shorthand for anti-scholasticism. The problem with calling Rolle anti-intellectual, as I will discuss later in this book, is his discussion of thinking and understanding, which, of course have an intellectual dimension. Further, there is a shorthand being used for emotion as not being intellectually based, as if suggesting that emotions cannot be learned, based in thinking, etc. Finally, in accusing Rolle of anti-intellectualism there is an implied suggestion that his mysticism is not "thought-out" and, therefore somehow less worthy of our attention. Yet, Rolle is often discussed as an able exegete, and his commentaries are also well received by scholars (then and now). There needs to be a new sense of emotive intellectualism. I would agree that Rolle is not Scholastic, yet, as many scholars agree he is influenced by the Victorines, Bernard of Clairvaux, and Francis. There must be some sense of the intellectual in his ability to synthesize his sources. Systematization in mystical work also must approach the inability to systematize.
18. Conor Cunningham uses this word to mean activity surrounding veiling (and unveiling): "for each object manifests a nubility, both revealing and hiding, because it is erotic and plenitudinal," p. 263.

19. Lawlor comments that phenomenology reflects the problem of language; as soon as the phenomenologist is reinserted into the world, they may lose the transcendent. There are two remedies: "on the one hand, he [the phenomenologist] can try to reduce the mundane meanings of the words he must use. [. . .] On the other hand, the phenomenologist can try to develop a technical language, a so to speak, 'nonworldy language'." Lawlor (with Fink) then laments that "Husserl never reflected on the possibility of a transcendental language," one that I think Rolle and other mystics are reflecting on within their own phenomenology. See Leondar Lawlor, *Derrida and Husserl: The Basic Problem of Phenomenology*. (Bloomington: Indiana University Press, 2002).
20. Lawlor, p. 13.
21. As John Caputo comments in his analysis of Heidegger's own mystical bent "a philosophy which is not open-ended and receptive to the vision of the mystic is a sterile rationalistic; and a mysticism which resists the clarifying reflection of the philosopher is an irrationalism which serves no purpose and accomplishes nothing." *The Mystical Element in Heidegger's Thought*. (New York: Fordham, 1986), p. 8. Caputo is suggesting then a balance to philosophy and theology. There is an openness that mysticism puts forth and a rationalism that (traditional) philosophy puts forth. It is the place where they meet where we may find Rolle's work.
22. Heidegger, *The Phenomenology of Religious Life*, p. 43.
23. Heidegger, *The Phenomenology of Religious Life*, p. 45.
24. Adam S. Miller, *Speculative Grace: Bruno Latour and Object Oriented Theology* (New York: Fordham University Press, 2013), p. 152.
25. Graham Harman, *Guerilla Metaphysics*. (Chicago: Open Court, 2005), p. 21.
26. For a discussion of intentionality in Derrida and the relationship between deconstruction and phenomenology see Lawlor, pp. 2–3.
27. Lawlor writes, "This relation to other means that whenever I intend something, it includes the possibility of absence or non-presence," p. 231.
28. Harman, *Guerilla Metaphysics*, p. 21.
29. Ahmed, p. 38.
30. Richard Rolle, *The Fire of Love*. Trans. Clifton Wolters (London: Penguin, 1972), p. 45.
31. Karma Lochrie, "The Language of Transgression: Body, Flesh, and Word in Mystical Discourse," in *Speaking Two Languages: Traditional Disciplines and Contemporary Theory in Medieval Studies*. Ed. Allen J. Frantzen. (New York: State University of New York Press, 1991), p. 128.
32. Rolle, *The Fire of Love*, p. 45.
33. Rolle, *Incendium Amoris*. Ed. Margaret Deanesly (New York: Longman, 1915), p. 308.

34. Rolle, *The Fire of Love*, p. 45,
35. Conor Cunningham, p. 135.
36. For a discussion of Scotus and univocity see Frank and Wolter's *Dun Scotus Metaphysician* and Peter King, "Scotus on Metaphysics." *The Cambridge Companion to Duns Scotus*. Ed. Thomas Williams (Cambridge: Cambridge University Press, 2003), pp. 15–69.
37. Graham Harman, *Guerilla Metaphysics*, p. 104.
38. Harman, p. 105.
39. Lawlor writes that "To conceive proximity ontologically means that one must recognize that being, in Heidegger, is nothing, is not a being, and is nameless. This necessity to say 'nothing' is why Derrida stresses Heidegger's metaphorics; *phainesthai*, shining, lighting, clearing, *Lichtung* as well as voice, listening are all attempts to say being, that is, presence in a more original sense than its metaphysical or ontic determinations based on the present. These metaphors are supposed to lead us to conceive 'the near' and 'the proper' 'before [*avant*] the opposition of space and time according to the opening of a *spacing* which *belongs* neither to time nor to space, and which dislocates, while producing it, any presence of the presence," p. 40.
40. Harman, *Guerilla Metaphysics*, p. 108.
41. Harman, *Guerilla Metaphysics*, p. 109.
42. Rolle, *The Fire of Love*, p. 45.
43. Rolle, *The Incendium Amoris of Richard Rolle of Hampole*, p. 146.
44. Rolle, *The Fire of Love*, p. 46.
45. Rolle,*The Fire of Love*, p. 45.
46. Rolle,*The Fire of Love*, p. 46.
47. Rolle, *The Fire of Love*, p. 46.
48. Heidegger, *The Phenomenology of Religion*, p. 245.
49. John Dun Scotus, "Concerning Human Knowledge" in *Philosophical Writings*. Trans Allan Wolter (Indianapolis: Hackett, 1987), p. 102.
50. Cunningham, p. 137.
51. Rolle, *Desyr and Delit* in *English Writings of Richard Rolle: Hermit of Hampole*. Ed. Hope Emily Allen (Gloucester: Allan Sutton, 1988), pp. 57–58.
52. As John Caputo points out in his analysis of Heidegger and mysticism: "mysticism is not opposed to thinking; on the contrary '...the most extreme sharpness and depth of thought belong to genuine and great mysticism'" (SG, p. 71). As well, "Mysticism dwells in the closest proximity to thought, in the region where representational thinking has been left behind and the Principle of Sufficient Ground has not influence. It is the mystic who teaches is to hear what the metaphysician can never detect. The mystic has 'thought' the relation of being and ground more 'sharply' and 'deeply' than the metaphysician," *The Mystical Element in Heidegger's Thought*, p. 73.

53. Rolle, *The Fire of Love*, p. 58.
54. Cunningham writes, "to know is, in a sense, to be towards an other—who is also the unknown; just as ultimate intelligibility I afforded to creation at the same time as it lies beyond it. [...] knowledge involves difference—otherness—and so it is ultimately love," p. 192.
55. For a discussion of the intertwining of memory and sensuality see Rosemary Drage Hale, "'Taste and See for God is Sweet': Sensory Perception and Memory in Medieval Christian Mystical Experience." In *Vox Mystica: Essays on Medieval Mysticism in Honor of Valerie M. Lagorio*. Ed. Anne Clarke Bartlett (Rochester: D.S. Brewer, 1995), 3–14.
56. Rolle, *Ego Dormio* in *Richard Rolle: Prose and Verse*. EETS. no. 293. Ed. S.J. Ogilvie-Thomson (Oxford: Oxford University Press, 1988), ll. 7–9.
57. Rolle, *Ego Dormio*, ll. 14–15.
58. Rolle, *Ego Dormio*, ll. 82–84.
59. Rolle, *Ego Dormio*, ll. 96–100.
60. Rolle, *Ego Dormio*, ll. 104–105.
61. Rolle, *Ego Dormio*, ll. 125–129.
62. Rolle, *Ego Dormio*, ll. 218–219
63. Rolle, *Ego Dormio*, ll. 222–223.
64. Rolle, *Ego Dormio*, l. 226.
65. Rolle, *Ego Dormio*, ll. 232–235.
66. Rolle, *Ego Dormio*, l. 249.
67. Rolle, *Ego Dormio*, ll. 309–315.
68. Another way to frame passive immanence is to think of Husserl's "passive synthesis." According to Lawlor, "passive synthesis implies that consciousness does not constitute or create its object, but rather receives and unveils it. Unveiling an 'already constituted' object, however, implies that a prior genetic process must have given rise to the object. But, this genetic process, in turn, too would have to have a passive layer and an 'already constituted' object, and so on. For Husserl, according to Derrida, a universal reason animate this infinite historic progression; teleological Reason animate all history with the Idea of an infinite task of knowledge," p. 26. Mystical phenomenology would not have a problem necessarily with the infinite regress as God would be the object already constituted, withdrawn, and veiled.
69. M.F. Wakelin, "Richard Rolle and the Language of Mystical Experience in the Fourteenth Century." *Downside Review* 97 (1979): 199.
70. Kotsko, *The Politics of Redemption*, p. 189.
71. Gordon Rudy, *Mystical Language of Sensation in the Middle Ages*. (New York: Routledge, 2002), pp. 7–8. See also Cunningham's discussion of *Dasein* as language, p. 140.
72. Rudy, p. 9.

73. In *Being Singular Plural*, Jean-Luc Nancy writes that "everything then passes *between us*. This 'between' as its name implies has neither a consistency nor continuity of its own. It does not lead from one to the other; it constitutes no connective tissue, no cement, no bridge. Perhaps it is not even fair to speak of a 'connection' to its subject; it is neither connected nor unconnected; it falls short of both; even better, it is that which is at the heart of a connection the *inter*lacing [l'entre*croisment*] of strands whose extremities remain separate even at the very center of the knot. The 'between' is the stretching out [*distension*] and distance opened by the singular as such, as its spacing of meaning. That which does not maintain its distance from the 'between' is only immanence collapsed in on itself and deprived of meaning," p. 5. Jean-Luc Nancy, *Being Singular Plural*. Trans. Robert D. Richardson and Anne E. O'Byrne. (Stanford: Stanford University Press, 2000).
74. Rolle, *Ego Dormio*, l. 70.
75. Rolle, *Ego Dormio*, ll. 96–97.
76. Jean-Luc Nancy writes "Christian identity is from the outset a construction through self-overcoming: the ancient law in the new law, the logos in the Word, the *civitas* in the *civitas Dei*, and so on" in "The Deconstruction of Christianity" in *Religion and Media*. ed. Hent de Vries and Samuel Weber. (Stanford: Stanford University Press, 2001), p. 119. Christian mysticism is another example of "self-overcoming" in that the mystic must overcome Church law in order to experience the divine without mediation, and at the same time, the mystic is central to Christian history as the sign of God's intervention into the world.
77. Rolle, *Ego Dormio*, l. 220.
78. See the Introduction of *Two Revisions of Rolle's English Psalter Commmentary and the Related Canticles*. EETS. no. 340. Ed. Anne Hudson (Oxford: University Press, 2012), p. xxvii.
79. Rolle, *The Fire of Love*, p. 93.
80. For a discussion of Rolle's use of tactile metaphors see Rosamund S. Allen, "Tactile and Kinesthetic Imagery in Richard Rolle's Works." *Mystics Quarterly* 13.1 (1987): 12–18.
81. Sara Ahmed, *Queer Phenomenology*. (Durham: Duke University Press, 2006), p. 1.
82. Ahmed, p. 9.
83. Rolle, *The Fire of Love*, p. 57.
84. Ahmed, p. 37.
85. Rolle, *The Fire of Love*, p. 47.
86. Lawlor, p. 234.
87. Rolle, *The Fire of Love*, p. 49.
88. Rolle, *The Fire of Love*, p. 51.
89. Rolle, *The Fire of Love*, p. 87.

90. Rolle, *The Fire of Love*, p. 88.
91. Rolle, *The Fire of Love*, p. 89.
92. Rolle, *The Fire of Love*, p. 89.
93. Rolle, *The Fire of Love*, p. 89.
94. Rolle, *The Fire of Love*, p. 92.
95. Rolle, *The Fire of Love*, p. 101.
96. Rolle, *The Fire of Love*, p. 99.
97. Rolle, *The Fire of Love*, p. 100.
98. Rolle, *The Fire of Love*, p. 109.
99. Rolle, *The Fire of Love*, p. 184.
100. Rolle, *The Fire of Love*, p. 184.

CHAPTER 4

Richard Rolle's Ecology of *Canor*: An Aesthetics of Desire

> *For what is more glorious than music, which modulates the heavenly system with its sonorous sweetness, and binds together with its virtue the concord of nature which is scattered everywhere? For any variation there may be in the whole does not depart from the pattern of harmony. Through this we think with efficiency, we speak with elegance, we move with grace. Whenever, by the natural law of its discipline, it reaches our ears, it commands song.*
>
> —Cassiodorus

Abstract Richard Rolle's concept of *canor* considers a divine sound ecology that works through Rolle's work. Rather than emphasize God's love visually as many mystics do, Rolle experiments with the ineffability of sound, an acousmatics, in order to express an ecological relationship, one in which the singer inhabits the sound of God and, thus, renders the body porous as sound permeates it. Rolle's use of the lyric reveals the enmeshed quality of singer, song, divinity, and body. In this way, Rolle's lyrics create environments that queer the body's relation to song. The gift of *canor* in Rolle's work creates a performative aspect to contemplative living. Rolle's experiment with sound and lyric open up a divine ecology that intermediates between singer and God.

Keywords *Canor* · Lyric · Acousmatics · Sound ecology · Soundscape

What if God is sound? This chapter examines the way in which Richard Rolle's song erases boundaries between bodies and experiments with enmeshment through an ecology of sound, one that resonates with Cassiodorus's own sense of a heavenly system of sweetness. Rolle's emphasis on *canor* in his texts suggests a kind of harmonics of the body with God and a mystical experience that queers the body and emphasizes the enmeshment of flesh and sound. By employing an immersive ecological poetic in his lyrics, Richard Rolle is experimenting with the love of Christ expressed in song and sound rather than visually, or as Mary Arthur Knowlton comments, "ecstatic expressions of the sweetness and joy that flooded his soul."[1] These "ecstatic" lyrics attempt to create an ecological event for the singer utilizing the name of Jesus. By singing the name, the boundary between singer and divinity is dissolved as song and sound themselves become inhabited environments.

In Chapter 2 I discussed Rolle's ontology and the conditions by which the hermit and their worldview was made visible. In Chapter 3, I built on Rolle's queer, ontological exploration of being to examine what the hermit experiences when God touches the soul. In this Chapter, I want to delve deeper into Rolle's sound phenomena focusing on the mystical experience of *canor*. By invoking the sounds of the Passion, conflating time and sound, and experimenting with the mouth of the lyricist by translating acousmatic[2] sound so that the body of the hermit becomes an instrument harmonizing with the divine, Rolle attempts to capture the panoply of emotion, action, and object surrounding devotion by singing it and responding in song. Rolle weaves past and present, sound and sight, Jesus and singer, into an immersive, divine soundscape. As Stuart Kaufmann phrases it, "the God we discuss [...] might be God as the unfolding of nature itself."[3] Kaufmann's metaphor underscores the becoming-nature of the divine within the lyric's performance itself. Song becomes the ecological moment *par excellence*, a moment that immerses various objects (singer, sound, air, text, and flesh) into an event in which bodily boundaries are erased and desire is mapped in ways that reveal queer drives.[4] The lyrical sound reveals that there is no outside in the connection between the body as instrument and the God-sound.

Recent work in medieval lyrics has charted the relationship between sound, song, singer, songbook, and context revealing an enmeshed genre of literature, one that is performative, changeable, and open.[5] Marisa Galvez's work on songbooks argues that there is a "tension between lyric as performed event (through both oral and written transmission) and the translation of this lyric into knowledge."[6] Galvez's work with the *Carmina Burana* and the *Libro de Buen Amor* unpacks the medieval lyric as a *sung* genre, as well as emphasizes the openness that performativity welcomes. Galvez remarks that the codices "are open enough for readers to use as they see fit: performed aloud, or studied silently from any point through one's own moral lens."[7] This lyric performativity suggests ways in which singer and song create ecological moments that reveal queer ways of living with and *as* sound in a non-normative spiritual praxis. With Tim Ingold, I call this attentiveness to sound a way to approach bodies as "ensounded."[8]

Three key ideas run as threads throughout this chapter: (1) Rolle utilizes sound ecology as a site of God's touch through lyrics that reconfigure the body of the singer to create divine harmony; (2) Rolle's lyrics translate acousmatic soundscapes, environments in which the experience of God as sound without clear origin is brought imminently to the mouth of the singer; and (3) in reconfiguring the mouth, in making sounds like angels, the lyric becomes a site of coexistence with the divine and thus a divine soundscape is created during the duration of the lyric.[9] In the previous chapter, I addressed the ways in which Rolle refigured the sonorous body in order to experience the divine. In this chapter, then, I want to emphasize Rolle's gift of *canor* and the way his lyrical work functions as a way to express the reader's and his own efforts to recapture the divine song through the singing of the lyric and theorizing the ensounded eremitic body within religious devotion, such as the reading of the *Psalms*. Rolle theorizes divine sound as a queer touch awakening the capability of the lyricist and singer that moves the performer to harmonize with God as a queer, mystical practice.[10] The whole body becomes receptive to sound; the eyes sing. This practice aims to stage the body's excess in love and saturate it with and as sound.

Soundscapes and Divine Sound

A soundscape is an aural-based landscape, an auditory environment that surrounds a listener and constructs space. In 2009 the composer, John Luther Adams, created a music installation in Alaska in which he utilized geological, meteorological, and magnetic data and tuned and transformed it into electronic sound.[11] In his "Forward" to John Luther Adam's composer journals compiled as *The Place Where You Go to Listen*, *New Yorker* music critic, Alex Ross, comments that Adam's work, composing with the atmospheric, geological, and ecological sounds of Alaska, reveals that:

> it is a forbiddingly complex creation that contains a probably irresolvable philosophical contradiction. On the one hand, it lacks a will of its own; it is

at the mercy of its data streams, the humors of the earth. On the other hand, it is a deeply personal work, whose material reflects Adam's long-standing preoccupation with multiple systems of tuning, his fascination with slow-motion formal-processes, his love of foggy masses of sound in which many events unfold at independent tempos.[12]

Thinking with Adam's project and considering how sound is transformed and tuned dependent on the instrument itself—Adam's work, for example, is set in a natural setting so that bird song or dog barks create a counterpoint to the percussion that seems to rise from the very setting—I turn to Richard Rolle's work with *canor* to think about the enmeshed ecology such divine lyrics may invoke, and how the body, as an instrument may produce divine sounds.

Medieval musical theory, or *musica speculativa*, defines music as "contemplation that serves the moral edification of the mind."[13] Influenced by the work of Boethius's *De Musica*, music is not just everyday music but "connotes harmony conceived broadly enough to encompass the relationships obtaining in the human body and psyche and governing the motions of planets."[14] This kind of harmonic enmeshment is explored in the work of Boethius, especially in his discussion of abstract qualities in the prelude to the *De Musica, The Book of Arithmetic*:

> Indeed these things themselves are incorporeal in nature and thrive by reason of their immutable substance, but they suffer radical change through participation in the corporeal, and through contact with variable things they change in veritable consistency.[15]

These "essences" are concordant with mathematical properties expressed in music. For Boethius, music was both speculative and moral, and these intertwining purposes derived from music's phenomenological pleasures, "for nothing is more consistent with human nature than to be soothed by sweet modes and disturbed by their opposites."[16] Boethius also comments on the psychological effects experienced in hearing music as they "affect and remold the mind into their own character."[17] Boethius gives examples of how certain groups of peoples, such as the Thracians or Lacedaemonians, delight in different kinds of music that harmonizes with their natures. For Boethius, music is transcendent in that it exists as a kind of eternal sound, but also an immanent sound, in that it appeals to various peoples depending on their nature and environment.

Boethius' speculations lead him to think about harmony and sound as available to reason and sensory perception. Perhaps the most important aspect to thinking about Rolle's own speculative hearing is the notion of harmony itself as "the faculty of considering the difference between high and low sounds using the reason and senses. For the senses and reasons are considered instruments of this faculty of harmony."[18] The use of the body as an instrument that must discern harmony by balancing sense perception with reason resonates in Rolle's work in terms of both harmonizing with divine transcendence and the sensory experience of immanence within the ecology of the lyric. In this way, Rolle is exploring a harmonic balance between these two mystical ideals, as well as considering his body as a queer, mystical instrument that shapes and amplifies that sound.

Rolle's mystical gifts are unique in that he does not privilege the scopic. His mysticism explores the aural gifts of God. The experience of song or *canor* is one of the highest mystical gifts. As in John Luther Adams's work, *canor* unfolds in ways both translatable and ineffable. *Canor* creates a kind of being, one that creates place and, then, surpasses it. As Andrew Albin wries, "*canor* emerges as constant sonorous coparticipation with the angelic choirs, a state of transcendent musical being."[19] Rolle writes in the *Incendium Amoris* at the moment of his receiving the gifts of God: "I heard, above my head it seemed, the joyful ring of psalmody, or perhaps I should say, the singing [...] I became aware of a symphony of song, and in myself I sense a corresponding harmony at one wholly delectable and heavenly."[20] In this initial receipt of *canor*, Rolle is made aware of space and the way that it is mimicked in his own biology. The space of the sacred church is transformed into an eternal space that is put in harmony with God. In his first experience, the musical song he hears above him transforms him internally: "my thinking turned into melodious song and my meditations became a poem, and my very prayers and psalms took up the same sound."[21] This transformation erases the boundaries between the external song and the internal song, or as Adam's frames the ecology of sound, "the totality of the sound, the larger *wholeness* of the music."[22] Rolle's body itself becomes a musical instrument beyond its initial sound capabilities and resonates with the chapel space itself to become a harmonious space.

Harmony in the form of enmeshed vibrations suggests both a local and cosmic allusion to complex systems of divine transcendence and immanence. The work of Alfred North Whitehead explores the power of vibrations in the power of creativity and novelty. For example, Alfred North Whitehead writes that a conceptual feeling is, "feeling an eternal object in the primary metaphysical character of being an 'object' that is to say, feeling its *capacity* for being a realized determinant of process. Immanence and transcendence are the characteristics of an object: as a realized determinant it is immanent; as a capacity for determination it is transcendent."[23] The lyric realized by Rolle is immanent; within it, God reveals Itself in a particular event. God and sound, however, are transcendent as they are both capacities and reveal themselves in a vibratory harmony within the immanent lyric itself. As Whitehead points out elsewhere, "God is the measure of the aesthetic consistency of the world. There is some consistency in creative action because it is conditioned by his immanence."[24] In pointing to creative action, Whitehead frames his argument of a God working in the world. As process philosopher, William Connolly, comments, "it is through the periodic acceleration of 'vibrations' within and between entities that novel formations emerge."[25] The transcendent God is a kind of capacity; the lyric then prehends (both positively and negatively) in order for God's creative immanence to appear and take a phenomenal sound shape.[26]

Rolle's *canor* anticipates the problem of the capacity of hearing and sound that the modern world is beginning to realize.[27] It also reflects the space for personal and private devotion opened up by exclusion of Christian worshippers from the Mass itself. As Patrick S. Diehl remarks, "the late medieval exclusion of worshippers from the actions of worship [...] was the end result of a process that began before the end of antiquity. This process had major effects on medieval religious lyric, creating a stillness in which lay piety, together with the vernacular could speak."[28]

The medieval religious lyric is a site to experience and experiment with new sounds, sounds that may be intermediaries between the divine and the personal. The lyric, with its attention to sound, alliteration, poetics, and performance, mark changing attitudes toward sound.[29] It is only recently that we have cultivated the technology to hear the sound of atoms, for example. There are sounds that are new, such as industrial or technological sounds, as well as "more materially mediated" sounds (stethoscopes, rooms, iPods).[30] The medieval lyricist speculates, then: like the sound of an atom, something beyond our capacity to hear, what kinds of sounds does God make? Or what kinds of sounds does the touch of God make the singer express?

Theologically speaking, listening has been a key concern for the Gospels. From Jesus's role as Word, to God's order for the disciples to "listen" to Jesus during the event of the Transfiguration,[31] there is a theological concern both with *not* listening because of distractions, as well as with preparing oneself to hear correctly in order to work toward harmony. God works in Rolle's song in both of these ways: to listen and to prepare oneself for harmony. The divine song takes a sound shape in Rolle's poems and commentaries on the *Song of Songs* as well as the *Psalms*.[32]

The lyric then is a "performative environment"[33] one in which the relationship between singer, audience, and song create a world and comment on that world.[34] Rolle's lyrics do two things within the realm of sound studies. The lyrics work as a kind of "exploratory listening" in which Rolle uses singing and hearing to explore sounds. As well, Rolle's lyrics work as a kind of "synthetic listening" in which we "focus on the polyphonic patterns of sound" such as we find in the work of Luther Adams.[35] In this way, sound can increase awareness; one's visual field can be restricted to the corners of peripheral visions; however, put on a pair of earphones and the soundscape increases exponentially.

Rolle's lyrics are an imperfect, by his estimation, commentary on the gift of *canor*. As Diehl comments, "medieval metaphysics and poetics work together to make closure look very much like an aberration or even a fault."[36] The lyrics cannot answer definitively what God sounds like or even if the contemplative is listening correctly; the lyrics are delicious failures. The performance of the lyrics, however, allows the discernment of a divine whisper within Rolle's divine ecology. The divine sound rendered into song and psalm is an order and an ordering. As Ann Astell points out, Rolle "reliteralizes" the *Song of Songs*, one of his most quoted sources.[37] This "reliteralization" allows Rolle to take on the role of the *sponsa Christi* in his works.[38] Amy Hollywood and Karma Lochrie have both pointed out the queer potential in utilizing the *Song of Songs* as a mystical rubric. However, each of their works centers on womens' responses to Jesus' feminized body.[39] Rolle's lyrical role of *bride* queers his role as singer in order to remap desire and experience the divine through sound. In this way, Rolle expresses what Tison Pugh in his investigation of the medieval lyric, calls "opportunities for queering authorial play through the contradictory conflation of private desires expressed in public discourse."[40] Rolle's body and Christ's body are queered, penetrating each other with sound. If the *Song of Songs* is a touchstone text for Rolle, his use of that text offers him an opportunity to reconfigure his relationship with the world so that his mystical experience of divine song becomes *a* world itself. Rather than focus on the *Song of Songs* in thinking of Rolle's *canor*, I want to think about Rolle's lyrics with the *Psalms* as a way to theorize the "tone of heaven."[41]

Rolle and the Tones of Heaven

Rolle translated and commented on the *Psalms* throughout his life and his work with the *Psalms* was clearly influential, as multiple versions exist adapted for a wider reading public and various audiences, including Lollards, after his death.[42] As Andrew Albin comments, "the *Psalms* act as a kind of bridge between worldly and angelic praise. [...] reciting the *Psalms* is a kind of lesser *canor*, stripped of its mystical, and musical, qualities."[43] The *Psalms* also connects the reciter with divine song through a metaphorization of their body into an instrument of sound.

In Rolle's *English Psalter*, Rolle theorizes the connections between song, books, and divine presence. Rolle begins his prologue by connecting spiritual comfort to those "at says or synges deuotly *the* psalmes in louynge of ihu crist."[44] Rolle moves on to think about the book as both an enclosed garden and a musical instrument. These metaphors work to gesture toward the power of song. In terms of the garden, the *Psalter* works to provide stability and comfort, a "paradyse ful of all appils" that provides soul with a "clere & pesful lyf."[45] The "garthen closed" that Rolle creates here is a metaphor for the Psalter's power. Much like his first experience of *canor*, the closed garden allows the body to harmonize with space.[46] It is within enclosure that freedom is most found, since the singing of the song allows the singer to be removed from the world.[47] It is the song "that delites the hertes & lerese the saule is made a voice of syngand and with aungels whaim we may noght here we menge wordis of louynge sa that worthily he may trow him aliene fra verray lyf wha sa has noght."[48] By singing the psalms, Rolle is indicating that the singer comes close to harmonizing with angels; this divine connection reveals an enmeshment with that which they cannot hear with human ears, but still reminds the singer that they are singing *like* the angels. It is the closest to angelic song that the singer can perform on earth; through sonorous articulation, the pattern of the divine is being heard and sung as it becomes legible in the *Psalms* themselves.

Rolle continues the metaphoric power of instrumentation in his discussion of the book as a musical instrument.[49] Rolle first provides his reader with an etymological explanation of why the psalter is thusly named: "this boke is cald the psautere the whilk nam it has of an instrument of musyke that in ebru is nablum in grek psautery of psallm that in inglis is to touche and it is of ten cordis & gifes the soun fra the ouerere thurgh touchynge of hend"[50] Rolle connects this etymological lesson to both the work of the Ten Commandments—connecting the chords and fingers to the work done by following the commandments—and to the messages contained in the psalms themselves:

> Thare in is discryed the medes of goed men the pynes of ill men the disciplyne of penaunce the waxynge in rightwise lif the perfeccioun of haly men, the whilk pass is til heuen the lyf of actyf men the meditacioun of contemplatifs & ioy of contemplacioun the highest that may be in man lifand in body & feland. Alswa what synne reues fra mannys saule & what penaunce restores.[51]

The ten chords of the psalter are touched by hand; as Rolle indicates this same kind of touching "gif soun fra vpward at the touchynge of oure hend"[52] when we work on earth. As in the previous passage, Rolle is connecting song with divine immersion; in other words, songs that the contemplative sings, and works that they do, connect them with the divine, whether they fully realize it or not. The *Psalter*, as a book, mimics the chords, not only in terms of the human work demanded by the Commandments but also in its very divisions, themselves containing the messages of both the Old and New Testament. This metaphoric enclosing allows the singer to pursue avenues to divine sound.

In "Psalm Five," Rolle contemplates the nature of the voice itself. Rolle asks that the "psalmodye of my mouth" be recognized. As Michael P. Kuczynski writes, the Psalter created a model for medieval writers in that the Psalms presented "a representative, ethopoetic voice expressed in the first person."[53] This voice allowed the writer to connect the individual with the Christian community itself. This conflation of "psalmodye" and mouth indicates again the power of the voice; the mouthed psalm will move the singer closer to the divine.[54] Rolle's call for understanding in the next sentence resonates with the "cry," which is the yearning of his heart. Rolle gestures toward the human voice's need to be interpreted by God; God can misunderstand the nature of the sound, as well. This cry is one of longing and joining. God must also recognize it.

For Rolle, the mouth and heart are joined. And, the singer seeks to know if his petition is heard. The faith intertwined with song is relevant here, since Rolle is suggesting that God may not hear or may misunderstand. If one sings a song in the darkness, does it make a sound? How will the singer know if they are heard? For Rolle it is when the light of grace comes after the darkness of sin "wystis a way."[55] The problem for the singer, then, is the voice's attachment to sin or darkness. Like other places discussed in this book, the hermit's sounds are born out of a space of adversity. This sin/darkness is contrasted with grace/morning, and in the morning the singer will stand. The voice that God hears and God responds to, however, is also corruptible both for the singer and for the voice itself.

Rolle admits that his preoccupation with slanderers or backbiters affects the ability to forgive and stand in God's presence. Rolle prays that God will lead him back to "consciens whare man see noght, bot anly god: and that consciens aghe noght to trow til man, lackand or louand, for he sees it noght: in the whilke oure way is rightyd till god."[56] As discussed previously, sight is deceiving; it is only in inner knowledge that truth is found. This need for self-knowledge is also reflected in Rolle's need to delineate good sounds from bad.

The problem of the voice, of course, is that it may mislead. The backbiters or slanderers have throats "lyknyd til a graue openand, for thai shew stynkand wordes that corumpis the herers."[57] Rolle wrestles with the idea that voice can also be handled by those who are corrupt. This connection between a corrupted voice and the grave reveals Rolle's concern with how we might be swayed by a false voice, one that slanders and flatters. A false sound that comes out of these doomed individuals is contrasted later with Jesus's name which is "hele and ioy" since noone "wondire if thai be in ioy of hele that lufs it."[58] As I will discuss later in this chapter, Jesus' name contains a sound of pure joy, a divine rhythm explored in Rolle's lyrics.[59]

Rolle's commentary on Psalm 32 perhaps best encapsulates his connecting song with a new way of living. As Rolle unpacks verse three: "synge til him a new sange, that is, dosaway all synn and clathis yow in new life and clen: and wele syngis til him with goed werkis in heghynge of voice."[60] Singing to and of God is a way to be with God. When one is performing works of mercy, Rolle indicates that it is a kind of song, one that God hears. Act and song are entangled, affecting God's hearing. In Psalm 64 Rolle translates the Latin "te decet ympnus in syon" as "god bicomes ympne in syon," in Zion God becomes a hymn.[61] Rolle's interpretation of this verse is that the word "ympne" means "louynge with sange" or "that he sings that lufis the verlaly." Rolle's movement from God as hymn to God as verb is key to the becoming-song that Rolle posits.

In this passage God is song, the act of singing, and the object of devotion for the singer. God flows in and around. In the act of singing, the singer loves. The singer sings who truly loves. Rolle's verbal gymnastics, placing God in various positions speaks to the power of the song-ecology. The song enmeshes one with God; as well, the song touches God and brings divinity closer.

This theorizing of song as a connection between sound and the work that the contemplative performs on earth places them within the Psalter, within an enclosed garden, that gives the singer the freedom to pursue divine harmony. As Rolle writes, "to synge, that is to life right-wisly"[62] is an immersion in divine harmonics. Life and song are joined for a glimpse of divine reward. Singing the psalms places the hermit in a position to voice God, to hear something of the divine presence. Their bodies provide an instrument in which to harmonize with the divine.

By voicing God as one would do in reciting the *Psalms*, Rolle provides a template for a divine sound within the lyrics. Rolle imposes an intrinsic order that reveals something of the divine world—in other words the lyrics are a sign of God's immanence working in Rolle's sound world. In thinking through the world of Rolle's song, his meditations found in the lyrics, provide some clue as to what this *canor* might sound and feel like and what it can do.

Rolle's Sound Ecology

Andrew Albin's work in Rolle's historical aurality serves as a springboard for my own analysis. For Albin, "aurality refers to the culturally determined condition and qualities of a sound event that shape its perception as an event that is 'given to be heard'."[63] A sound ecology will "valorize and urge auditors toward specific aural configurations, protocols for hearing, and mappings of sound experience upon the body that serve the interests of specific cultural actors."[64] Ecologically speaking concepts of medieval nature had to do both with the concept of being and the innate capacity of a thing, *kind*.[65] This combination of Platonic and Aristotelian concepts of nature can be found in the work of Thomas Aquinas, for example. In his commentary on *Physics II* he writes, "nature is nothing other than the rationale of a certain art, i.e. the divine one, by which the objects themselves are moved toward their determined end."[66] Nature reveals the hand of the Divine; their enmeshment suggest a divine ecology.

Borrowing from the work of Timothy Morton, ecology is a way to think about coexistence. As Morton writes in *The Ecological Thought*, "ecology includes all the ways we imagine how we live together. Ecology is profoundly about coexistence. Existence is always coexistence. No man is an island. Human beings need each other as much as they need an environment."[67] The environment is a thinking-through of the ways we live together. The lyrics in Rolle's work help us to see how community is formed through a kind of life outside of traditional community building.[68] A symphony orchestra must inhabit the score in order to live together on the stage. The violinist and the percussionist coexist with their instruments, the air, the audience, the conductor's baton, the building, the financial flow from donors—all constituting an environment that is changeable, mutable even, but requires thinking about coexistence to survive. The symphony orchestra requires a kind of eco-praxis. It is a reflection of the phrase "in-tune," one which captures the Latin and the Greek connotation of *symphonia*, "the special ability of music to symbolize an agreement."[69] For Rolle an ecological community is forged in soundscape.

In this way the lyric is a kind of encounter.[70] As Susan Crane comments, "when saints speak with wild animals and change their behavior, they are experimenting with their environments. Nature comes into configuration around the saint, interpreting with monastic culture and facilitating its projects."[71] The animal is the great Other in these encounters; the encounter itself calls into question normative *human* behaviors, as Crane indicates here, by calling into question who we talk to, what it means to experiment with our surroundings, and exactly how the enactment of certain behaviors, like monastic rules, may reveal surprising behaviors lifted out of the monastic milieu. In this way, the song, lifted out of the normative ecclesiastical setting, reveals surprising relations. The ecological encounter within song asks us to rethink grammars, response, meaning, and endings.

As well, we can think about performance, as that done with song, in terms of what Wendy Arons and Theresa J. May call "ecodramaturgy" which is the marrying of ecology and drama in order to think through "drama in relation to earth processes" which "stretches any notion of epic theater to the far reaches of human attention."[72] Cornelia Hoogland writes about her use of "sound ecology" with urban students who may not have the experience of green spaces on an everyday basis. She used the play *Woods Wolf Girl*, a retelling of Grimm's fairy tale, in order to draw attention to the historical presence of wolves in the park, for example, by providing audio in earphones for the students. As Hoogland outlines, albeit in a contemporary theater context, using concepts of "sound ecology" push the participant so that they are "not simply hearing a story about somebody else, they are walking where the narrator instructs them to walk, seeing what the narrator instructs them to see, and implicitly, feeling and thinking what the performance of the audio wants them to experience. In this way, participants are encouraged to 'become' or 'merge' with the characters and thus experience the story and the setting more deeply."[73] Hoogland's pedagogical use of sound can be likened to medieval mystical writers own use of directives in order to achieve an effective response in their audience. In this way, the mystic is creating a sound world, one that jerks the reader, listener, speaker, or singer out of a familiar world and adding layers of sensory directives in order to deconstruct ontological concepts of the real and suggest the divine in the immanent.

As Morton writes, "reframing our world, our problems, and ourselves is part of the ecological project. This is what *praxis* means—action that is thoughtful and thought that is active."[74] The making of the divine into song for Rolle is a praxis, an active way to reconsider the relationship between God and man beyond a pure anthropomorphism. Rolle's use of the lyric is an ecological thought, a "reading practice" that "makes you aware of the shape and size of the space around you (some forms, such as yodeling, do this deliberately). The poem organizes space [...]. We will soon be accustomed to wondering what any text says about the environment even if no animals or trees or mountains appear in it."[75]

Rolle's lyrics survive in a number of different forms in a number of different manuscript types. Some lyrics are individually collected as are those in CUL MS Dd.5.64 and Longleat MS 29. Some lyrics are excerpted as in the Carthusian Miscellaney, BL MS Add 37049 aimed at a religious audience. Robert Thornton (d. 1465) copied some of Rolle's lyrics into a manuscript for lay readers, Lincoln Cathedral MS 91, while other lyrics exist in BL Add 31042, which is a two-volume household book containing recipes, romances, and miracles. Other lyrics exist within Rolle's prose works such as the *Incendium Amoris* or the *Ego Dormio*.[76] While I will be focusing on those from CUL MS Dd.5.64, I will also be considering those embedded in the *Ego Dormio* to consider the affect of sound within the stand alone lyric, as well as the effect prose has on lyrical ecology. I will conclude this chapter by looking at the Carthusian Miscellany BL Add 37049 to consider how medieval readers may have rendered Rolle's mystical song and its performance.

I am concerned with a reading practice that takes into account the song as an ecological thought. As Albin points out, "for Rolle, then, the essential, ravishing quality of *canor* in the irreducible experience of its specific soundedness and heardness—in other words, in its aurality."[77] I want to first consider a lyric that Rolle adopted from his *Incendium Amoris* that Hope Emily Allen has given the title "A Song of the Love of Jesus." From here, I want to meditate on the other lyrics, but this lyric situated in a text that proposes the link between the gifts of contemplation and the power of the lyric will provide us with a framework to think about Rolle's lyrics as "sounded" and the way Rolle proposes to live and experience within Christ's melody.[78]

This lyric addresses not only the nature of Christ's love but also the way that love reaches out to the singer and turns the world inside out. The singer declares, "Luf es lyf þat lastes ay, þar it in Criste es feste."[79] This kind of love defies timescales: a love that lasts "ay" or always. The lyric wrestles with the problem of how to establish real Love and how it is realized in Christ. Since the love we know on earth is marked by mortality, this lyric experiments with scales of time and queer temporality. Rolle is implying this Love is based in the here, since it is in Christ, God who has taken on flesh, that "Love" is "feste." In contemplating a lasting Love, Rolle is considering the gap between love and life, or, more specifically a love that is a lasting life and a love that quickly fades. This becoming-love must be separated out from other kinds of love that separate the singer from the community. Can Love be an ethic, one which takes into account the flesh, while forcing the singer to go beyond it, to think of it as something more? This kind of love is exemplified in the fire that "sloken may na thyng."[80] Love is an excessive fire, one that nothing can put out and, therefore, everything is subsumed in it.

The metaphoric power of Rolle's love is evident here. The sound of fire is connected with Love's embrace. Rolle is suggesting this ecological moment, not in an apocalyptic way, but as a fire that creeps into all crevices. Nothing can "sloken" it—the sibilance of the consonant blend "sl" gestures toward the crepitation itself. It is the sound of fire touching the object as it prepares to consume and reveal, to take it into itself, as well as reveal the object's being not otherwise noticed. In other words, Rolle creates a Love that offers the object a new being; imagine words, like those written on the One Ring in J.R.R. Tolkien's *Lord of the Rings*. Once fire touches the ring, it reveals itself in ways that merely by being in a pocket or on a chain go unseen. Only Love can gesture toward the unseen; the sound of fire is a sound of revelation.

As Rolle contemplates this love that takes up everything, he notes that love is also here on earth, but it is often "sle."[81] This "sl" consonant blend is repeated. Craftiness is closest to the idea of a kind of lust—Rolle predicts the reader asking about the nature of this lust, but Rolle claims to not know any lust to compare this kind of love to. For Rolle true Love runs, it is fleet, but as it is realized on earth it is heavy and brief. Rolle compares love to the briefest of beauties: "fleschly lufe sal fare as dose þe flower in May,/And lastand be na mare þan ane houre of a day."[82] The brevity of love is a revelation in one sense, the singer can hear it happening right there in the field, but it is bracketed by time. Rolle wants to emphasize the everlasting nature of Love, the flower is only a quick glimpse of Love in time.

Once Rolle considers that love is available on earth, albeit briefly, Rolle proposes a kind of love that erases the taint that may be attached to (earthly) love. In terms of this lyric, the goal is to make the lyric a kind of "glew." Hope Emily Allen offers the translation of this word as a glow or joy and in the line of the lyric "his mourning turned til joy ful bright, his song intil glew," it makes sense as sadness will be turned into a bright joy. The song in this line is not a mourning, it is a *joining*, and thus, turning the song into a glow is not its *opposite*, rather, it is a turning of sound into a kind of light.[83] The song is a penetrating act; it allows the singer to become aware of their boundlessness.[84]

What if we also read the word "glew" with its other Middle English nuances as "glue"? The lyric becomes a binding agent to God.[85] I am punching up the nuances here to underscore the power of the lyric to erase the boundary that is placed between God and singer by "sle" love. Earlier in this lyric, Rolle emphasizes how "luf copuls" God and singer.[86] Glowing/gluing is multivalent in its sound to suggest the boundaries between natural processes, in this case light and sound, can be erased and other configurations can be attached.

The theme of binding and coupling run throughout this lyric. Rolle scales up from the body to the song itself turning the singer inside out to experience the love around them. The body itself is constituted by love: "lufe byndes blode and bane."[87] On the one hand the internal bodily structure of the singer is a sign of love's binding power; on the other hand, it is also the sign of their inability to love fully. As Rolle comments, "when þair bodys lyse in syn, þair salws mai qwake and drede/For up sal ryse al men, and answer for þair dede."[88] To lie in sin is in direct contrast to the "bedde of blysse it gase ful nee" offered up at the beginning of the lyric.[89]

The body could be in repose in the bed of bliss, but instead it is too rooted in care. The nearness of the bed ("gase ful nee") makes the singer realize the possibilities before them in the opportunity of the song itself. Instead, the singer's "syghe" is full of lust, pride, and care.[90] This worldly sigh is in direct contrast with the song itself.

The lyric itself is a song of Christ's love. In Love, one can sing joy.[91] The *potenta* of the song is highlighted here. Rolle is demonstrating the potential song of Christ—the one the singer can grasp echoes of on earth through the gift of *canor* and glimpsed at in the *Song of Songs* and *Psalms*. As Pike argues, music "can be identified with idea, and is *a priori* in the sense that potential music governs the actual music."[92] Inside the lyric, we see the way that the earthly love is critiqued, the body is turned to sighing over worldly care instead of singing; the singer themselves inhabits a different joy. The lyric as performed by the singer creates a world in which the song inhabits the singer, makes them turn toward everlasting love. The final line of the lyric reads, "Jhesu, gyf us grace, as þou wel may, to lufe þe withowten endyng."[93] This wish is the glue/glow of the song itself. As the lyric progresses, and the singer enters into the contemplation of the nature of their soul, the song is inhabited further by the singer. To go inside the lyric is to find Love.

The scribe divided the line in half in the Thornton manuscript. The first half of the lyric ends with the "gleu" line. As I have discussed, it is in that section that the singer turns from sighing and sobbing over Jesus to finding the lover in their heart that allows them to inhabit the song itself—to be bonded with Christ. The dividing up of the lyric highlights the change that the singer is making as they progress through the song. It is in the next section that Rolle aligns Christ with love and melody: "If þou will lufe, þan may þou syng til Cryst in melody./þe lufe of hym overcomes al thyng; þarto þou traiste trewly."[94] If the singer enters into Love, then all things are overcome and melody is formed. To "traiste trewly," whether Love, Christ, or the melody, aligns the singer with Christ's sound, the sound of the Crucifixion itself. It is this sound that Rolle has in mind as he sighs and sobs "bath day and nyght."[95] But, it is Love that allows him to live with this mourning and joy. Mourning and joy are kinds of sound that immerse the singer in the divine event.

In his commentary on Psalm LXXXV, Rolle explains the verse "inclina domine aurem tuam and exaudi me: quoiam inops & pauper sum ego" as a plea for Christ to hear him: "helde thin ere lord and here me."[96] Rolle petitions Jesus to hear how He is the one who will rescue him from poverty;

Christ is his only hope. The larger point is the plea for Jesus to *hear* Rolle. In the same way, the singer must listen. In a companion commentary to this Psalm exploring building a community based on hearing and being receptive to one another's sounds, Rolle also comments on Psalm XC. In that Psalm, Rolle contemplates the cry of Christ on the cross: "the cry of his brennad desire come til me and in that I sall here him, gifand him that he askis for I am with him in tribulacioun."[97] In this commentary, the community of Jesus and the singer is cemented in sound—hearing Christ in tribulation assures Christ that the singer is with Christ in his woe and suffering. Thus, sound touches each party, assuaging and comforting.

In this same lyric Rolle also contemplates entwined chronology of "þat swete chylde" and the Jesus "nayled apon þe tre."[98] There is a conflict between the evils of earth and the love that the world can offer. In other words, the very contemplation of the time of life brings both mourning and joy. Rolle invokes a queer temporality in that sound of Christ's woe. While the tree becomes a sign of torture and death, the melody, the song becomes a sign of the Love that will overcome all. They exist in the same breath. It is also Love that transforms into Jesus by the end of the lyric. As Rolle writes in an echo of the first stanza: "Jhesu es lufe þat lastes ay, til hym es owre langyng./Jhesu þe nyght turnes to þe day, þe dawyng until spryng."[99] The natural processes of night and day, dawn into sunrise, are infused with Jesus. But each needs the other—in order to turn into day, the night is necessary. For the joy to order the world, to bring a love that lasts always, the sounding of mourning is necessary. The sweet child needs the Crucifixion and the Crucifixion needs the sweet child. This is love everlasting, not eschewing the natural processes, but understanding their enmeshment, touching back and forth through time. In this lyric, Jesus is that becoming; while Rolle begins the poem considering the nature of Love itself, the twist at the end of the lyric is to find out that the singer was singing of Jesus-Love all along. In this song, the singer has become the song; in the singing, the singer has *become* with Christ's love. There is a *symphonia* of singer/song/Christ. Rather than wasting away in sighs, one must immerse oneself in song. The bed of bliss is closer than one thinks; Rolle is commending his singers to sing it.

The name of Jesus is key in Rolle's lyrics in that it echoes John Caputo's concept of name-as-event. For Caputo "taking the name of God as the name of a call rather than of a causality. [...]"; it is "the name of an event transpiring in being's restless heart, creating confusion in the house of being, forcing being into motion, mutation, transformation, reversal."[100]

By invoking the name of Love, the singer has entered into the consideration of themselves in the song and melody of God. In a "Song of Love-longing to Jesus," Rolle addresses the relationship between love and Jesus but rather than meditate on the nature of that love, as in the previous lyric, Rolle meditates on the event that causes that love: the Crucifixion. The lyric is bookended by violent acts. At the beginning, Rolle asks Christ to "take my heart intil þy hand, sett me in stabylte" and "thyrl my sawule with þi spere, þat mykel luf in men has wroght."[101] In both these cases Christ's hand and spear enter into Rolle creating a locality of singer and divine presence. In the first line, it is to settle his heart—a theme that Rolle repeats in many of his writings. The stability of the heart allows it to open so that Christ can take up residence and, in that "indwelling," the soul and Christ become one. In the second piercing, the spear pierces the soul and Rolle seems to be implying that this piercing has been done before and, in fact, the piercing itself is the action that has opened the human to love. As Jesus was pierced by the lance of the Romans, the soul is pierced by Jesus and in that act, love is made or "wroght." In the second piercing, the "thyrl," the spear pierces the soul and Rolle plays with the mouthing of the word as a kind of reverse piercing. The interdental fricative configuration of the voiced "th" in the word "thyrl" made by scraping the tongue between the teeth to form the word is like the removal of the spear from the wound itself. The lips make a wound shape and the tonguing of wounds reveals the intimacy inimical to the movement of the mouth, to sound out this pain and wrench the lips to connect the singer with Christ.

The latter event of the poem is the scene of the Crucifixion itself.[102] As Jesus has first pierced Rolle and in that event awoken or caused Love, we can imagine the spear as the linking object, something that erases the boundaries between Christ and Rolle. However, the middle third of the poem relates how Rolle lives a life of longing—and the love of Jesus will resolve this longing: "I sytt and syng of lufe-langyng, þat in my hert is bred."[103] The song is a result of the piercing; it is as if the removal of the spear has opened up a new song: that of love-longing. Rolle is lamenting the loss of the spear. The love-longing song, the hole itself, becomes the lyric. The lyric explores the soundscape of the Crucifixion.

The meditation on the Crucifixion begins with Christ bursting forth. If the first image of the lyric is of Rolle being pierced inwardly, Christ ends the poem with a flowing out: "His bak was in betyng, and spylt hys blessed blode; þe thorn corond þe kyng, þat nailed was on þe rode."[104] Notice the repetition of "b" and the "th" consonant blends. The "b"'s recreate the lashes, the "th"'s repeat the five piercings of Christ on the cross. The Passion is related in two lines, but Rolle underscores the sound of the piercing of Christ as a way to show his overabundance. The flowing out of Christ in the lyric is another way to remove the boundary between singer and Christ. Christ also becomes the song as He is bound with the flowing rhyming words: fode/stode/blode/rode become the pattern of the Passion itself.

Let us look closely at this stanza's rhyme. The first and third, "fode" and "blode," refer to the Eucharist itself. It is out of the second and forth words: "stode" and "rode" from which we get that Eucharistic event. Jesus is beaten and Crucified; the Eucharistic feast of body and blood (or "aungel fode") are a reminder of that event. In other words, Rolle has contained the connection between Eucharist and Crucifixion in four rhyming words and the lyric becomes a piercing of that event itself.

As well, the mouthing of these four rhyming words mimics the biomechanics of eating. This mimesis of the bloody event is a sound-meditation on the pierced and open body of Christ on the cross. In the next stanza, Rolle witnesses the bloody "syde" and the deep wounds.[105] It is from these deep wounds that "his blode gan downe glyde."[106] In the piercing of the body and the flowing of the blood, Rolle has reversed the initial piercings seen earlier in the poem. This red event is one that erases, in its sound and liquidity, any separation of lover and Christ, since it is in the song, the blood, and the body that we find Love. In the "fode" and the "blode" that the Christian ingests in the Eucharist, Christ is taken in and absorbed. As Rolle writes, it is the "aungels brede was dampned to dede, to safe ours sauls sare,"[107] in other words it is the body of Christ as bread or food for sore souls. The longing that Rolle wishes to be resolved is found in the stable heart that Rolle so desires Christ to handle, and is solved in the mouth's participation with the Eucharist itself.

The love-longing that Rolle inhabits in this life is assuaged in the erasing of boundaries found in the holy feast of body and blood. In meditating on the Crucifixion, Rolle creates an ecology of the holy event mirrored in the ritual of the Eucharist. The Eucharist is a reminder of Christ in the everyday—the basic needs of food and drink are both blessed and reminder of the name of Christ as Love.

The name of Jesus, thus, contains an event that situates the singer in the light. In a "Salutation to Jesus," Rolle invokes Christ's name 11 times in 28 lines. The invoking of the Name, an invocation that becomes Rolle's calling-card, creates a world in which he must learn to give. Christ has already suffered for the singer, as he imagines half way through this lyric, "Allas, my God es, als a thefe, nailed til þe rode./Hys tender vayns begns to brest, al rennes of blode./Handes and fete with nayles er fest; þat chawnges mi mode."[108] As the body is burst in song, this contemplation brings the singer closer to the body. The fixed nature of the body and its bursting fix the singer until he draws away to consider himself: it is this act of violence, this sacrifice, that changes the singer's mood.

But the body of Christ here becomes an object that moves Rolle to right loving because within "fandyng" or temptation the body is "fast" or found.[109] As in the previous lyrics, Rolle is situating the event of the Crucifixion within the lyric. The song becomes a song and the assemblage that Rolle has built here is one in which the event creates Love and grace. In every event of a trial that the singer faces it is the body that comes to mind, so that in finding the body of Christ, in remembering the pain, Christ supports the singer. The symbiosis at work here, and what makes this lyric unique from the other two, is the invocation of the name "Jhesu." Before beginning the meditation on the fixed body, Rolle first inhabits the name. The Name is called to remind Rolle of Christ as creator, savior, and son.[110] As the lyric is centered around opening the singer to the song and to realize Christ in the song, the repetition of the Name in this lyric, as Caputo writes, "solicits and disturbs what is there, an event that adds a level of signification and meaning, of provocation and solicitation to what is there, that makes it impossible for the world, for what is *there*, to settle solidly in place, to consolidate, to close in upon itself."[111] It is the name of Christ in this lyric that allows Rolle to combine song and light in a new illuminated, sonorous world.

It is worth noting here how Rolle scales down Christ's roles: beginning with Christ as creator to his coming in the flesh. It is Christ in the flesh, immanent, on the Cross, that Rolle is able to experience love, and, in turn, scale himself up toward divine unity. Again, the lyric explores a queer temporality—as the roles of Christ are sung they exist at the same time immersing the singer in divine time. To work through the grace that Christ grants on the Cross during these trials, the singer will be lead into the light.[112] It is through the fixed, nailed body that Rolle recognizes his ability to love correctly. The fixed body and flowing blood mark a strong contrast of stability and flow. This is likened to Rolle's seated contemplation while the Love suffuses him from God's seat in his heart. As Rolle comments in this lyric, "forþi þai sitt my hert ful nere, þat I forgete þam noght."[113] The nearer that Rolle "sits" in relation to Christ, the clearer he can remember or meditate on Christ's pain and within that pain, that sorrow, Rolle can love.[114]

An anomaly in Rolle's lyrics is the prose lyric, "Gastly Gladnesse," contained in the Longleat manuscript. If the other lyrics discussed have strong alliteration, bold rhyme schemes and ordered lines, the prose lyric is a block of text that emphasizes spiritual joy resting on alliterative technique only. "Gastly Gladnesse" addresses the love-longing that Rolle has discussed in earlier poems; however, in this prose lyric the spiritual joy that he experiences is contrasted with the absence of it—joy has been taken away from him and life is now open. But it is the Love that makes him compose this lyric: "lufe makes me to melle and joy gars me jangell."[115] As Allen mentions in the notes to this lyric, Rolle uses "jangell" negatively elsewhere.[116] "Melle" and "jangell" here, however, reflect Rolle's loss of boundaries of self in the joy of song that constitutes his life on earth. While Rolle waits for his life to end, he must find a way to live with the longing. In other words, with the spiritual joy he experienced Rolle tasted everlasting life or "dede war dere."[117] Now it is absent. The word Rolle repeats twice in this poem is "lyghtsumnes" or an ease of spiritual joy. This "lyghtsumnes" is contrasted with "hevynes" of melancholy.[118] Rather than let melancholy sit too near, and we can extrapolate here and think about the only thing Rolle wants to sit near is Christ, he must maintain spiritual joy.

As Rolle writes "bot in gladness of God evermare make þow þi gle."[119] In gladness of God the singer will find joy. The world is part of this joy and they must bring that joy to the forefront. In the act of melting—dissolving heavy boundaries that keep us from God—they become singers. The joy they experience is connected to the act of the "jangler"—by allowing song to flow out of them so that they transform their ecology, as well as experience God's immanence and their interconnection with God. The ecology of the lyric makes them aware of how the song connects them, creating a space for God and human to sing one another. In the song the singer gives form to God and in giving form to God they reliteralize, with Rolle, the ability to dissolve themselves and sing.

The Materiality of Sound

In terms of manuscript representations of song, I want to conclude this chapter with a discussion of the Carthusian Miscellany, British Library Additional MS 37049.[120] This Carthusian Miscellany has drawn much excellent critical attention of late, therefore, I only want to focus on a specific leaf,

f. 30v, in order to suggest how Rolle's lyrics may have been received and how a late medieval audience represented the lyric at work.[121] This leaf is unique to BL MS Add 37049 for a number of reasons. Because of its size, nearly three-quarters of the page, the dramatic impact of the lyric is fully explored by the illustrator/scribe. As well, the lyrics written on the banderole are repeated in the prose work itself creating a link between lyric and prose. And, finally, even though banderoles are used elsewhere in the book, these scrolls relate a very dynamic, dialogic song, as opposed to a conversation or a speech to another figure.[122]

In f. 30v, a reclining figure, identified as a portrait of Rolle, reclines on a field of green. In his hand is a parchment. His eyes look up to a blue and red sunburst which contains the Virgin Mary holding the baby Jesus in front of a field of stars. The lyrical dialogue the two figures exchange revolve around the *Psalm* which opens Rolle's *Ego Dormio*: "Ego dormio et cor meum vigilat." Reading down the page, the banderoles draw our eyes downward in a zigzag pattern. In other words, the banderoles dramatize a call and response until we read the bottom of the leaf where the scribe has begun *Ego Dormio* in prose. The Virgin Mary begins by singing a promise, "If þou my true lufer wil be/ My selfe to reward I sal gyfe þe." The reclined figure responds with a translation of the first lines of *Ego Dormio* re-translated into a Middle English couplet: "I slepe and my hert wekes to þe/Swete Ihesu þe son of Mary fre." The rhyming couplets of each banderole match the other indicating a kind of musical duet. They are singing to one another.

But to underscore thinking about the song as an ecology, a "wilderness lyric," notice how everything is enmeshed.[123] The reclining figure, despite claiming he is sleeping, has his eyes open and aimed at the Virgin Mary and Jesus, who are equally gazing back at him.[124] The rounded green ground seems to swallow the figure, absorbing him in his meditation. As well, the blue sunburst encloses the Virgin Mary and child, but banderole, sun beams, and arms reach out to the other. There is a lyrical drama here as the space between them, though short, cannot be broached, except through song. The time of Jesus as child and the now is represented. The lyrics open relationships in time. The sunburst contains depth: the Virgin Mary and Jesus are poking through space. Their backdrop is a starry night sky, as if the power of the song has ripped open the very page to make a divine connection between the two singers.

The banderole shapes create complementing U's, linking each other. The reclined figure's banderole unfurls back on itself, repeating the lines in Latin: "ego dormio et cor meum vigilat." The Latin opening to the Psalm creates a bridge to the prose beneath the singer and beneath the green field. The scribe has chosen to not only repeat the line, he contains the phrase in another field—in this case, a red box, to draw attention to its linguistic power: "I sleep, but my heart is awake." As the song is exchanged between the reclining figure and the Virgin Mary and child, the reader/singer of the text repeats that song; the song and phrase becomes the link between the reader as they perform the lyric and the book itself as it draws the reader closer. The song draws attention to the power of the image and the power of the song enmeshes the reader with the book itself. The reader is further drawn into the text as they will go on to read Rolle's *Ego Dormio* on the following leaves—lyric and prose, illumination and words, reader and book are further glued through song creating a queer community through time, sound, and space, on the page and in the repose of a divine, lyrical, and readerly performance.

The ecology of Rolle's lyric makes us aware of how song connects, creating a space for God and human to sing one another. Rolle's lyrics experiment with the form of God; in giving sound-form to a relationship with the divine, Rolle queers the contemplative, eremitic body. Rather than focus on the scopic quality of visionary experience, Rolle experiments with soundscapes in order to immerse the singer in divine sound. The eremitic body becomes an instrument used to make sounds that vibrate with the divine.

Notes

1. Mary Arthur Knowlton, *The Influence of Richard Rolle and of Julian of Norwich on the Middle English Lyrics*. (Paris: Mouton, 1973), p. 51.
2. For a discussion of acousmatics see Brian Kane, *Sound Unseen: Acousmatic Sound in Theory and Practice* (Oxford: Oxford University Press, 2014). Kane defines acousmatic sound as "the cause of the noises—whether seismic, chemical, carbuncular, or divine—remain unseen; its sound is an audible trace of a source that is invisible to the listener," p. 3.
3. Stuart A. Kaufmann, *Reinventing the Sacred: A New View of Science, Reason, and Religion* (New York: Basic Books, 2008), p. 287.
4. Dianne Chisolm writes of the queer desire of the desert that informs my thinking here where "non-reproductive sex is a primary force of nature," p. 360. Dianne Chisolm, "Biophilia, Creative Involution, and the Ecological Future of Queer Desire." *Queer Ecologies: Sex, Nature, Politics, and Desire.* Eds. Catriona Mortimer-Sandilands and Bruce Erickson. (Bloomington: Indiana University Press, 2010).

5. For a wide-reaching history of the medieval lyric see Peter Dronke, *The Medieval Lyric* (Cambridge: D.S. Brewer, 1996). For a discussion of medieval poetics that informs this analysis see Paul Zumthor, *Towards a Medieval Poetics*. Trans. Phillip Bennett (Minneapolis: University of Minnesota Press, 1992).
6. Marisa Galvez, *Songbook: How Lyrics Became Poetry in Medieval Europe* (Chicago: University of Chicago Press, 2012), p. 9.
7. Galvez, *Songbook*, p. 19.
8. Tim Ingold, *Being Alive: Essays in Movement, Knowledge, and Description*. (London: Routledge, 2011), p. 139.
9. As Bruce Holsinger writes, "the sonorous body performed an essential role within poetic practice, theological and devotional discourse, liturgical performance, pedagogical transmission, and visual culture throughout the medieval era." Bruce W. Holsinger, *Music, Body, and Desire in Medieval Culture: Hildgard of Bingen to Chaucer* (Stanford: Stanford University Press, 2001), p. 3.
10. For a discussion of music as a relation with God see Èlisabeth-Paule Labat, *The Song That I Am: On the Mystery of Music*. Trans Erik Varden. (Collegeville, MN: Cistercian, 2014).
11. For a film introduction to Adam's project see John Luther Adams—*A Sonic Geography of Alaska*. Youtube video. http://www.youtube.com/watch?v=vvPUlgUWsz8.
12. Alex Ross, "Forward," in John Luther Adams, *The Place Where You Go to Listen: In Search of an Ecology of Music* (Middletown, CT: Wesleyan University Press, 2009), p. x.
13. Jan Herlinger, "Music Theory of the Fourteenth and Early Fifteenth Centuries" in *Music as Concept and Practice in the Late Middle Ages*. ed. Reinhard Strohm and Bonnie J. Blackburn. (Oxford: Oxford University Press, 2001), p. 293.
14. Herlinger, "Music Theory," p. 293.
15. Calvin Martin Bower, *Boethius' The Principles of Music: An Introduction, Translation, and Commentary*. George Peabody College for Teachers, diss., 1967, p. 24.
16. Bower, *Boethius' The Principles of Music*, p. 32.
17. Bower, *Boethius' The Principles of Music*, p. 34.
18. Bower, *Boethius' The Principles of Music*, p. 295.
19. Andrew Albin, "Listening for *Canor* in Richard Rolle's *Melos Amoris*. *Voice and Voicelessness in Medieval Europe*. Ed. Irit Ruth Kleiman. (New York: Palgrave MacMillan, 2015), p. 178.
20. Richard Rolle, *The Fire of Love*. ed. and trans. Clifton Walters. (London: Penguin, 1972), p. 93.
21. Rolle, *The Fire of Love*, p. 93.

22. John Luther Adams, *The Place Where*, p. 1.
23. Alfred North Whitehead, *Process and Reality* (New York: The Free Press, 1978), p. 239.
24. Alfred North Whitehead, *Religion in the Making* (Cambridge: Cambridge University Press, 2011), p. 86.
25. William Connolly, *The Fragility of Things: Self-Organizing Processes, Neoliberal Fantasies, and Democratic Activism* (Durham: Duke University Press, 2013), p. 156.
26. As Jonathan Hsy comments, "if we think of language not only as a vehicle of speech, sound, and writing, but also as a phenomenon that occupies space and disperses itself across locations, then any language might be considered a living organism with its own agency," p. 37. My idea of Rolle's lyric as a sound with its own agency to create parallel's Hsy's. See Jonathan Hsy's *Trading Tongues: Merchants, Multilingualism, and Medieval Literature* (Columbus: Ohio State University Press, 2013).
27. For a discussion of Rolle's use of *canor* rooted in Augustinian musicology see Robert Boenig, "St. Augustine's *Jubilus* and Richard Rolle's *Canor*." *Vox Mystica: Essays on Medieval Mysticism in Honor of Professor Valerie M. Lagorio* (Cambridge: DS Brewer, 1995), 75–86.
28. Patrick S. Diehl, *The Medieval European Religious Lyric: An Ars Poetica* (Berkeley: University of California Press, 1985), p. 43.
29. For a discussion of historical sound see Peter A Coates, "The Strange Stillness of the Past: Towards an Environmental History of Sound and Noise." *Sound Studies: Critical Concepts in Media and Cultural Studies*. Vol. I Ed. Michael Bull (London: Routledge, 2013), 277–308.
30. For a discussion of the frontiers of sound study, see Trevor Pinch and Karin Bijsterveld, "New Keys to the World of Sound" in *The Oxford Handbook of Sound Studies*. Eds. Trevor Pinch and Karin Bijsterveld (Oxford: Oxford University Press, 2011), p. 5.
31. See Matthew 17: 5. It is worth noting here that the emphasis is on the sound of God and hearing Jesus in this verse as cloud has descended and the disciples are unable to experience God except in sound. Sound introduces the disciples to the awe of divinity; it is only when they are prostrate that Jesus then touches them and they look up to see Jesus alone. This sensory order reveals the primacy of the introduction of divinity as experienced through sound and then the acquaintance of the other senses to Jesus.
32. For a discussion of Rolle's use of the *Song of Songs* see Denis Renevey, "Encoding and Decoding: Metaphorical Discourse of Love in Richard Rolle's Commentary on the First Verses of the Song of Songs." *The Medieval Translator 4* Ed. Roger Ellis and Ruth Evans (Binghampton: Medieval and Renaissance Texts and Studies, 1994), 200–217.
33. Galvez, *Songbook*, p. 35.

34. For a discussion of the participatory element in religious lyric as well as the debate over the definition of lyric see Patrick S. Diehl, *The Medieval European Religious Lyric* (Berkeley: University of California Press, 1985) especially pp. 20–21 and 22–30.
35. For a full discussion of "modes of listening" see Pinch and Bijsterveld, "New Keys," p. 14.
36. Diehl, *Medieval European Religious Lyrics*, p. 120. For an overview of key themes in medieval English lyrics see Christiana Whitehead, "Middle English Religious Lyrics" in *A Companion to the Middle English Lyric* (ed. Thomas G. Duncan. Cambridge: D.S. Brewer, 2005), 96–119 and Douglas Gray, *Themes and Images in Medieval English Religious Lyric* (London: Routledge, 1972).
37. Ann W. Astell, *The Song of Songs in the Middle Ages* (Ithaca: Cornell University Press, 1990), 106–107. For a discussion of the exegetical genre connected to the *Song of Songs* see E. Ann Matter, *The Voice of My Beloved: The Song of Songs in Western Medieval Christianity* (Philadelphi: University of Pennsylvaia Press, 1990). Also, Peter Dronke, "The Song of Songs and Medieval Love-Lyric." *The Bible and Medieval Culture*. Ed. W. Lourdaux and D. Verhelst (Leuven: Leuven University Press, 1979), 236–262.
38. Astell, p. 118.
39. See Amy Hollywood, "Queering the Beguins: Mechtild of Magdeburg, Hadewijch of Anvers, Marguerite Porete." *Queer Theology: Rethinking the Western Body*. Ed. Gerard Loughlin (Malden, MA: Blackwell, 2007), 163–175. Karma Lochrie, "Mystical Acts, Queer Tendencies." *Constructing Medieval Sexuality*. Ed. Karma Lochrie, Peggy McCracken, and James A. Schultz (Minneapolis: University of Minnesota Press, 1997), 180–200.
40. Tison Pugh, *Queering Medieval Genres*. (New York: Palgrave MacMillan, 2004), p. 21.
41. William F. Pollard, "The 'Tone of Heaven': Bonaventuran Melody and the Easter Psalm in Richard Rolle." *The Popular Literature of Medieval England*. Ed. Thomas J. Heffernan (Knoxville: University of Tennessee Press, 1988), p. 253.
42. For a discussion of Rolle's *English Psalter* and its adaptations see Anne Hudson's *Two Revisions of Rolle's English Psalter Commentary and the Related Canticles*. EETS. no. 340 (Oxford: Oxford University Press, 2012). As Hudson comments in her introduction, "critics suggested that three revised versions should be recognized, and associated all of them, with varying degrees of certainty, with the Lollards. In general terms, as will emerge, both of these suggestions appear to be reasonable," p. xxiii. For a discussion of Richard Rolle as a biblical

commentator see J.P.H. Clark, "Richard Rolle as a Biblical Commentator." *Downside Review* 104.356 (1986): 165–213.
43. Andrew Albin, *Auralities: Sound Culture and the Experience of Hearing in Late Medieval England.* PhdDiss. (Brandeis University, 2011), p. 151.
44. Richard Rolle, *The Psalter or Psalms of David and Certain Canticles.* Ed. H.R. Bramley (Oxford: Clarendon P, 1884), p. 3.
45. Rolle, *Psalter*, p. 3.
46. For a discussion the aural properties of "earcons" found in sacred spaces see Barry Blesser and Linda-Ruth Salter, "Ancient Acoustic Spaces" in *The Sound Studies Reader.* Ed. Jonathan Sterne. (London: Routledge, 2012), 186–196.
47. For a discussion of architecture and ambient medieval sound see Sheila Bonde and Clark Mannes, "Performing Silence and Regulating Sound: The Monastic Soundscape of Saint-Jean-Des-Vignes." *Resounding Images: Medieval Intersections of Art, Music, and Sound.* Ed. Susan Boynton and Diane J. Reilly. (Turnhout: Brepols, 2015), 47–70.
48. Rolle, *Psalter*, p. 3.
49. For a discussion of the power of Psalter translations to morally educate the community, see Michael P. Kuczynski, "The Psalms and Social Action in Late Medieval England" in *The Place of the Psalms in the Intellectual Culture of the Middle Ages.* ed. Nancy Van Deusen (Albany: State Univerisity of New York Press, 1999), 199–214.
50. Rolle, *Psalter*, p. 3.
51. Rolle, *Psalter*, p. 3.
52. *Rolle, Psalter*, p. 3.
53. Michael P. Kuczynski, *Prophetic Songs: The Psalms as Moral Discourse in Late Medieval England* (Philadelphia: University of Pennsylvania Press, 1995), p. 122.
54. Rolle, *Psalter*, p. 18.
55. *Rolle, Psalter*, p. 18.
56. Rolle, *Psalter*, p. 20.
57. Rolle, *Psalter*, p. 20.
58. Rolle, *Psalter*, p. 21.
59. For a descriptive overview of the lyrics see Rosemary Woolf's seminal *The English Religious Lyric in the Middle Ages* (Oxford: Clarendon, 1968).
60. Rolle, *Psalter*, p. 114.
61. Rolle, *Psalter*, p. 222.
62. Rolle, *Psalter*, p. 334.
63. Albin, *Auralities,*p. 14.
64. Albin, *Auralities,* p. 14.
65. For an examination of language and ecology in a different sense than my own see Tim William Machan's *The Ecology of Middle English* (Oxford:

Oxford University Press, 2003) in which he utilizes ecology to describe language usage across groups and spaces in order to account for language evolution.
66. Qtd. from Ludger Honnefelder, "The Concept of Nature in Medieval Metaphysics" in *Nature in Medieval Thought: Some Approaches East and West*. Ed. Chumaru Koyama (Leiden: Brill, 2000), p. 84. For a complete discussion of Greek philosophical antecedents in the work of Aquinas, Henry of Ghent, and Duns Scotus see Honnefelder's article, especially pp. 89–92. For further discussion of Thomas Aquinas' ecology see Willis Jenkins' *Ecologies of Grace: Environmental Ethics and Christian Theology* (Oxford: Oxford University Press, 2008), especially Chapter 7, "Environmental Virtues" in which Willis argues that Aquinas offers a counter-biology in order to reveal "virtue in light of the sanctifying share given humans in the divine uses of creation (naming, praising, glorifying)," p. 134.
67. Timothy Morton, *The Ecological Thought* (Cambridge: Harvard University Press, 2010), p. 4.
68. As Maria Galvez writes, "since medieval songbooks translate performative, oral, and auditory experiences of lyric poetry, they are useful for thinking about how archival objects relate to the medium and social conditions in which the lyrics are performed, just as modern poetry continues to be anthologized, and literary traditions are made and unmade through the practice of the songbook—the very process of making lyric poetry," p. 217. Rolle's lyrics appear in various manuscripts and excerpted in others—they are constantly in process as they are moved from context to context, for example, as in the Carthusian Miscellany BL MS Add 37049, as I will discuss later in this chapter.
69. William T. Flynn, "'The Soul is Symphonic': Meditation on Luke 15:25 and Hildegard of Bingen's Letter 23" in *Music and Theology: Essays in Honor of Robin A. Leaver*. Ed. David Zager (Lanham, MD: The Scarecrow Press, 2007), p. 2.
70. In using encounter, I am borrowing from Susan Crane's work in *Animal Encounters: Contacts and Concepts in Medieval Britain* (Philadelphia: University of Pennsylvania Press, 2013).
71. Susan, Crane, *Animal Encounters*, p. 5.
72. Wendy Arons and Theresa J. May, "Introduction" in *Readings in Performance and Ecology* (ed. Wendy Arons and Theresa J. May. New York: Palgrave MacMillan, 2012), p. 4.
73. Cornelia Hoogland, "Sound Ecology in the Woods: Red Riding Hood Takes an Audio Walk" in *Readings in Performance and Ecology* (ed. Wendy Arons and Theresa J. May. New York: Palgrave MacMillan, 2012), p. 189.
74. Morton, p. 9.
75. Morton, *The Ecological Thought*, p. 11.

76. For a discussion of Rolle's oeuvre see Hope Emily Allen, *Writings Ascribed to Richard Rolle: Hermit of Hampole* (New York: D.C. Heath, 1927); Ralph Hanna, *The English Manuscripts of Richard Rolle: A Descriptive Catalogue* (Exeter: University of Exeter Press, 2010); and, for an argument as to chronological order of Rolle's work, see Nicholas Watson, *Richard Rolle and the Invention of Authority* (Cambridge: University of Cambridge Press, 1991). For a general discussion of the problems of medieval lyric and their collection and editing see Julia Boffy, "Middle English Lyrics and Manuscripts" in *A Companion to the Middle English Lyric* (ed. Thomas G. Duncan. Cambridge: D.S. Brewer, 2005), 1–18.
77. Albin, *Auralities,* 144. For a discussion of performance of English Monophony and other medieval musical styles see *A Performer's Guide to Medieval Music.* Ed. Ross W. Duffin. (Bloomington: Indiana University Press, 2000). In Paul Hillier's discussion of "English Monophony," he discusses a variety of ways to sing the un-notated medieval English lyric, such as declamatory or equal syllabic style. Hillier's argument dovetails with my own in terms of sound experience when he writes, "the more one sings such music, the less arbitrary this process appears as one develops an innate sense of articulating the text and allowing the music to breathe, without doing violence to each other," p. 184.
78. Albin, *Auralities,* p. 145.
79. Richard Rolle, "A Song of the Love of Jesus," *English Writings of Richard Rolle, Hermit of Hampole.* Ed. Hope Emily Allen. (Gloucester: Alan Sutton, 1988), l. 1.
80. Rolle, "A Song of the Love of Jesus," l. 6.
81. Rolle, "A Song of the Love of Jesus," l. 9.
82. Rolle, "A Song of the Love of Jesus," ll. 57–58.
83. Rolle, "A Song of the Love of Jesus," l. 72.
84. As Alfred Pike argues in his *A Theology of Music,* "I regard music as a means of penetration to the reality behind all appearances." Alfred Pike, *A Theology of Music* (Toledo, OH: Gregorian Institute of America, 1953), p. x.
85. In the MED, however, the earliest use of glue is from John Gower, dated much later than Rolle: (a) (a1393) Gower CA (Frf 3) 5.3603: "Sche tok him thanne a maner glu.of so gret vertu That where a man it wolde caste It scholde binde anon so faste That noman mihte it don aweie."
86. Rolle, "A Song of the Love of Jesus," l. 12.
87. Rolle, "A Song of the Love of Jesus," l. 54.
88. Rolle, "A Song of the Love of Jesus," ll. 61–62.
89. Rolle, "A Song of the Love of Jesus," l. 11.
90. Rolle, "A Song of the Love of Jesus," ll. 59–60.
91. Rolle, "A Song of the Love of Jesus," l. 8.
92. Pike, *A Theology of Music,* p. 48.

93. Rolle, "A Song of the Love of Jesus," l. 96.
94. Rolle, "A Song of the Love of Jesus," ll. 67–68.
95. Rolle, "A Song of the Love of Jesus," l. 69.
96. Rolle, *Psalter*, p. 311.
97. Rolle, *Psalter*, p. 333.
98. Rolle, "A Song of the Love of Jesus," ll. 73, 86.
99. Rolle, "A Song of the Love of Jesus," ll. 41–42.
100. John Caputo, *The Weakness of God: A Theology of the Event* (Bloomington: Indiana University Press, 2006), p. 8 and 9.
101. Rolle, "A Song of Love-Longing to Jesus," ll. 4 and 6.
102. The liturgical connection in this lyric is evident as the worship of the Mass is centered on the Eucharist, a memento of the act of the Crucifixion. For a discussion of the liturgical connections to medieval lyric see Douglas Gray's discussion of liturgy and lyric in *Themes and Images in the Medieval English Religious Lyric* (London: Routledge and Kegan Paul, 1972), especially Chapter 2, "The Inherited Tradition, pp. 4–17.
103. Rolle, "A Song of Love-Longing to Jesus," l. 29.
104. Rolle, "A Song of Love-Longing to Jesus," ll. 35–36.
105. Rolle, "A Song of Love-Longing to Jesus," ll. 37, 38.
106. Rolle, "A Song of Love-Longing to Jesus," l. 40.
107. Rolle, "A Song of Love-Longing to Jesus," l. 44.
108. Rolle, "Salutation to Jesus," ll. 18–20.
109. Rolle, "Salutation to Jesus," l. 27.
110. Rolle, "Salutation to Jesus," ll. 1–4.
111. Caputo, *The Weakness of God*, p. 39.
112. Rolle, "Salutation to Jesus," l. 28.
113. Rolle, "Salutation to Jesus," l. 24.
114. As Timothy Morton comments on the plight of coexistence, "don't just do something—sit there. But in the mean time, sitting there will upgrade your version of doing and sitting," *The Ecological Thought*, p. 125.
115. Rolle, "Gastly Gladnesse," ll. 9–10.
116. See note p. 52, l. 10 (144): "Rolle uses *jangle* usually in an unfavourable sense."
117. Rolle, "Gastly Gladnesse," l. 6.
118. Rolle, "Gastly Gladnesse," l. 11.
119. Rolle, "Ghastly Gladnesse," ll. 12–13.
120. For a color version of this folio page see http://www.bl.uk/manuscripts/Viewer.aspx?ref=add_ms_37049_f030v.
121. For a discussion of the illustrators of BL Add MS 37049 as amateurs drawing on Carthusian sources and aimed at Carthusians and the devotional aspects of the illustrations see Julian M. Luxford, "Percept and Practice: The Decorations of English Carthusian Books" *Studies in Carthusian*

Monasticism in the Late Middle Ages. Ed. Julian Luxford (Brepols: Turnout, 2009), 225–267. For a discussion of the representation of music in manuscripts see Nicholas Bell, *Music in Medieval Manuscripts* (Toronto: University of Toronto Press, 2011).

122. For other examples of the use of banderoles in this manuscript compare f30v to f19r, f20r, f25r, f27v (where the banderoles are blank), f29v (where the couplets do not rhyme with each other), f36r, f48v, and f54v. In each case, the banderoles are more indicative of other kinds of speech patterns (sermon, monologue, etc.) than any kind of song. As Jessica Brantley writes, the lyrics in this Miscellany "can provide a clearer idea of how a late-medieval meditative poetics was informed by ideas of performance." Jessica Brantley, *Reading in the Wilderness.* (Chicago: University of Chicago Press, 2007), p. 123. For a collection of the images from BL Add. MS 37049 see *An Illustrated Yorkshire Carthusian Religious Miscellany British Library London Additional MS. 37049.* Ed. James Hogg. (Salzburg: Institut Fur Anglistik Und Amerikanistik, 1981).
123. Brantley discusses this image as well highlighting the dialogic quality of the page, but does not chose to analyze it in terms of a sound ecology. See Brantley, p. 138.
124. In his repose and open-eyed state, this possible portrait of Rolle can be likened to the top of a *transi* tomb. In this way, his death pose allows him access to the paradise as it is opened before him in the starry night beyond the Virgin's sunburst. The *transi* tomb is iconographically replicated many times in BL Add MS 37049 as a way to remind the monks to contemplate their death. For a full discussion of the moribund concerns of the Carthusians see M.V. Hennessy, "The Remains of the Royal Dead in an English Carthusian Manuscript, London, British Library, MS Additional 37049" *Viator* 33 (2002): 310–354.

CHAPTER 5

Epilogue: Three Vignettes

Coda

BUFFY:
I touch the fire and it freezes me
I look into it and it's black
This isn't real
But I just want to feel

SPIKE:
I died so many years ago
You can make me feel

ANYA, DAWN, GILES, TARA, WILLOW, AND XANDER:
Where do we go from here?

Buffy the Vampire Slayer, 6.7, "Once More, With Feeling"

Abstract Richard Rolle's own queer touch reaches into a future he did not know. From the nuns of Hampole who campaigned unsuccessfully for his sainthood, to Margery Kempe who internalizes Rolle's schema after hearing his works read to her, to Hope Emily Allen and her work to spearhead a Rolle canon, to this book and this author, Rolle touches us through time suggesting ways to bend our identities, to find an erotic divinity in our queer senses.

Keywords Hope Emily Allen · Fire · Queer touch · Transgender

As the cast of *Buffy the Vampire Slayer* sing in the musical episode written by Joss Whedon entitled "Once More, with Feeling," "where do we go from here?" Having been enchanted by the demon, Sweet, to sing their most hidden feelings, and thus revealing how they have felt about recent occurrences (including Buffy's own resurrection), the characters admit their confusion about the future. Once song has revealed all, once music has expressed the depths of the heart, what is there left to do?

Richard Rolle's own queer touch reaches into a future he did not know. From the nuns of Hampole who campaigned unsuccessfully for his sainthood, to Margery Kempe who internalizes Rolle's schema after hearing his works read to her, to Hope Emily Allen and her work to spearhead a Rolle canon,[1] to this book and this author, Rolle touches us through time suggesting ways to bend our identities, to find an erotic divinity in our queer senses.

Daughters of Fire

In her recent memoir *Living with a Wild God*, Barbara Ehrenreich thinks through a mystical experience she had when she was 17. Now in her mid-70s, Ehrenreich relates how when she was 17 in a desert town called Lone Pines "the world flamed into life."[2] Ehrenreich writes

> There were no visions, no prophetic voices or visits by totemic animals, just the blazing everywhere. Something poured into me and I poured out into it [...]. It was a furious encounter with a living substance that was coming at me through all things at once, and one reason for the terrible wordlessness of the experience is that you cannot observe fire really closely without being part of it.[3]

Ehrenreich's divine experience is marked by a Rollean *fervor* that we've explored in this book. Ehrenreich loses all sense of time; she even loses her sense of place to find herself eating in a diner with her family surprised by the sudden return of the "mundane [...] back to its old business of turning out copies of itself."[4] Ehrenreich did not know how to talk about this experience, putting off writing this memoir until she was much older. In the mode of a Julian of Norwich, Ehrenreich waits for over 50 years to shape the text and the experience.

Her description of the emotional impact of this flaming-event is important, as her mystical world of flame echoes that of the medieval lay mystic, Margery Kempe. While Kempe is in Leicester, she relates the experience of a "fyer of lofe [...] so yern in her hert that sche myth not kepyn it prevy [...]

it cawsyd hir to brekyn owte with a lowed voys and cryen merverylowslyche and wepyn and sobbyn."[5] This fire-inspired love bursts from Kempe, paralleling Ehrenreich's own overflowing experience. Ehrenreich calls it "ecstasy": "ecstasy would be the world for this but only if you are willing to acknowledge that ecstasy does not occupy the same spectrum as happiness or euphoria, that it participates in the anguish of loss and can resemble an outbreak of violence."[6] Ehrenreich's mystical experience touches back to Kempe's—as Kempe leaves the church a man asks her why she is crying so much. Kempe answers, "Syr [...] it is not yow to telle."[7] The emotional impact not chartable on a traditional emotional spectrum, the ecstasy of a divine touch, the losing of boundaries of the self to different configurations of space and time, the queerness of a desire not oriented toward any creature, all speak to the power of a divine experience that opens a world unrealized within the habits of the day-to-day. And despite their attempts to render it into language, there is that much more that is "not yow to telle." Ehrenreich draws our attention, much like Kempe, much like Rolle, to the fact that another world exists alongside the world that our senses are normatively configured to experience.

Although Ehrenreich does not point to Rolle as a source for understanding her experience (she explores and then rejects the medieval mystic Meister Eckhart), her divine experience is markedly queer. God is never a clear cause, neither is God ever anthropomorphized in her contemplations, rather, she suggests, the divine experience is irreducible to an ecstatic pull, one that lingers throughout her life. Ehrenreich's experience posits an open-object, an opening self, and the ebbs and flows of wanting. The point when the world bursts into flame always exists for her, and one may speculate how Ehrenreich's biography becomes subsumed in those flames—what would happen if she had let herself back into the flame?

THE SCHOLAR'S SWEETNESS

The fire swallows it all. Even biography. Records for Rolle are scant. What we have of his life is found in various Yorkshire records and the narrative of a life that is the *Miraculum*. But even his *Miraculum* does not conform to a hagiography. Rolle moves around too much, preaches from the margins of society too much. Even the posthumous miracles performed around his Yorkshire grave fall into three specific categories: the intercession of the Virgin Mary for various injuries, the saving of children from accidents, and the curing of the disabled.[8] All of these miracles are local. This emphasis on locality is important, for it reveals both the attempt to shape Rolle's hagiography and also reveals the ways in which he does not fit. The attempt at hagiography suggests less of the way in which his life conforms to the genre and more of how truly queer Rolle was in his form of living.

As I am suggesting throughout this book, the work of Rolle attempts to mine the surprise of the divine. In the Carthusian Miscellany, BL Add. 37049, Rolle's initial experience as related in the *Incendium Amoris* is Englished into a poem with short lines calling God to "Þi luf in to me sende/þat I may with þe lende/In ioy withouten ende."[9] It is the surprise of love that Rolle desires to live with, one that fulfills his desire when he asks earlier in the verse, "my hert when shal it bryst." Filled with love, the heart will no longer be able to contain Christ's indwelling, resulting in a bursting out. Love immerses the self from within, as the flame fills the cracks.

Despite the unknowable, openness of life, we continue to attempt hagiography. Hagiography invites us to shape a life, in an attempt to relate that life to the future. This book has immersed me in the touch of writers, scholars, and academics who have come before, inspiring me to make marks on the page, the writing process itself becoming a kind of immersive sweetness.

If Rolle has touched me deeply, enough to want to spend years researching and writing about him, the work of Michel Foucault has been with me throughout my academic career, proving foundational to my thinking as a scholar, writer, and queer. As David Halperin writes of Foucault in his *Saint Foucault*:

> As far as I'm concerned the guy was a fucking saint. Not that I imagine Foucault to have led either a sexually or a morally perfect life. In fact, I know almost nothing about his life beyond what I've read in three recent biographies [...]. I never met Foucault myself. I never laid eyes on him. My relation to him is indirect and secondary: like my relation to virtually every other great writer, ancient or modern, that I have studied, it is entirely mediated, imaginary, and—why bother to deny it?—hagiographical. But if Foucault did not have to lead a perfect life in order to qualify as an object of my worship, I certainly consider him to have led an intellectually and politically exemplary life [...]. Moreover, Foucault's acute and constantly revised understanding of his own social location enabled him to devise unsystematic but effective modes of resistance to the shifting, discursive conditions which circumscribed his own practice.[10]

Foucault and Rolle have touched throughout this book. Their need to shift, change, and create unsystematic modes of being that challenge normative political, religious, and domestic practices flow throughout. So, this book, too, ends up being a kind of queer hagiography of Rolle, one that celebrates his refusal to systematize, his need to open the body, his resistance of imposed binaries, his queer touch across time, and his suggestion of an alternate way of performing a spiritual *praxis* of ecstasies. *Fervor*, the fire-heart, becomes a strategy of resistance to a rote religiosity. *Dulcor* becomes a touch to immerse the self and turn the body onto the divine presence in the world. *Canor* becomes a form of relations that lose the trappings of normative desire and bend the self to harmonics previously unheard. As we consider the ways in which people both historical and present use religion and desire, absorb it in their bodies, model news ways of looking at the intersections where the material and the spiritual converge, we may think of Rolle, too, as Halperin's "fucking saint," an imperfect, desiring, hermit, modeling a queer body/self-relation with all of its shapes and forms of love.

Song's Erasing Touch

In North Carolina's Second Extra Session of 2016, Session Law 2016–3 House Bill 2 (HB 2) was passed. The law,[11] aimed at forcing transgender people to use the bathroom of the biological sex that is listed on their birth certificate no matter their own identification, became a touchstone of controversy for its hateful, discriminatory impetus as it was aimed at overturning Charlotte, North Carolina's own non-discrimination ordinance. Conservative politicians, such as Governor Pat McCrory who signed the bill into law, claimed that this bill was protecting citizens; however, the bill leads to impossible problems for transgender people. For example, the bill requires transgender people to use the bathroom that matches the biological sex listed on their birth certificate, but "of the total number of transgender people, there are significant proportions that have not undergone sex reassignment surgery, often due to the expense as well as medical risks. So transgender people who look and act like their preferred gender may not have had the surgery that would have allowed for their birth certificates to be changed."[12] McCrory and other politicians assume imposed, rigid categorization and binaries are easy answers to the beauty of the open-ended nature of bodies, gender, and sex.

Perhaps the loudest outcry against HB2 has come from musicians. Bruce Springsteen, Pearl Jam, Boston, Ringo Starr, Demi Lovato, and Ani DiFranco, as well as others, have cancelled their concerts in North Carolina in protest. Other musicians, such as Father John Misty, have donated the proceeds from their concerts to anti-HB2 organizations. Perhaps the most poignant protest came from the transgender lead singer of Against Me!, Laura Jane Grace, who burned her birth certificate at the band's concert in Durham, North Carolina on May 15, 2016. On her *Instagram* page, Grace writes, "Burn Gender Burn. Gender Inferno!"[13]

Fire swallows it all. Grace's protest through music and fire spark a conflagration that burns away the normative laws that dictate the categorization of being. It is significant that Grace burned her real birth certificate, a document that demands we match binary categories, as North Carolina was demanding it to be used as a normative marker of being—the birth certificate becomes another form of documentation, one Foucault reminds us is part of the trail of paperwork that makes a discipline of our being. Fire burns away these categories. The fire of protest, of love, erases these normative restrictions. Rolle's legacy combusts with Grace's protest, burning in our need to open the body past these normative boundaries, sweetly touching the resistance against imposed binaries as they reveal their brittleness and dissolve, singing the queer self that loves in excess, the notes rendering new selves into creation.

Notes

1. For a discussion of Hope Emily Allen's work on Rolle see John C. Hirsh, *Hope Emily Allen: Medieval Scholarship and Feminism* (Norman: Pilgrim, 1985), and for an exploration of Allen's queer relationships with time, see Carolyn Dinshaw, *How Soon is Now?: Medieval Texts, Amateur Readers, and the Queerness of Time* (Durham: Duke University Press, 2012), especially Chapter Three: "In the Now: Margery Kempe, Hope Emily Allen, and Me."
2. Barbara Ehrenreich, *Living with a Wild God* (New York: Twelve, 2014), p. 116.
3. Ehrenreich, p. 116.
4. Ehrenreich, p. 117.
5. *The Book of Margery Kempe*, ed. Lynn Staley (Kalamzoo: TEAMS, 1996), ll. 2610–2612.
6. Ehrenreich, p. 116.
7. *The Book of Margery Kempe*, l. 2615.
8. See Comper, *The Life and Lyrics of Richard Rolle*, Appendix I, p. 311–314.

9. Qtd. from Comper, *The Life and Lyrics*, Appendix II, p. 316.
10. David M. Halperin, *Saint Foucault: Towards a Gay Hagiography* (Oxford: Oxford University Press, 1995), pp. 6–7.
11. General Assembly of North Carolina, Second Special Session 2016. Session Law 2016-3. House Bill 2. http://www.ncleg.net/Sessions/2015E2/Bills/House/PDF/H2v4.pdf.
12. Fact Check: McCrory's "Myths vs Facts" email on HB2 http://www.wral.com/fact-check-mccrory-s-myths-vs-facts-email-on-hb2/15605025/.
13. Cimaron Neugebauer, "Singer of punk rock band Against Me! burns birth certificate in protest of HB2," http://kutv.com/news/entertainment/singer-of-punk-rock-band-against-me-burns-birth-certificate-in-protest-of-hb2.

BIBLIOGRAPHY

A

Adams, John Luther. *A Sonic Geography of Alaska*. Youtube video. http://www.youtube.com/watch?v=vvPUlgUWsz8.

Agamben, Giorgio. *The Highest Poverty: Monastic Rules and Form-of-Life*. Trans. Adam Kotsko. Stanford: Stanford University Press, 2013.

———. *The Kingdom and The Glory: For a Theological Genealogy of Economy and Government*. Trans. Lorenzo Chiesa. Stanford: Stanford University Press, 2011.

Ahmed, Sara. *Queer Phenomenology*. Durham: Duke University Press, 2006.

Albin, Andrew. *Auralities: Sound Culture and the Experience of Hearing in Late Medieval England*. PhD. Dissertation, Brandeis University, 2011.

———. "Listening for *Canor* in Richard Rolle's *Melos Amoris*". *Voice and Voicelessness in Medieval Europe*. Ed. Irit Ruth Kleiman. New York: Palgrave MacMillan, 2015. 177–197.

Alford, John A. "Biblical Imitatio in the Writings of Richard Rolle." *ELH* 40.1 (1973): 1–23.

Allen, Hope Emily. "Introduction." *English Writings of Richard Rolle: Hermit of Hampole*. Gloucester: Alan Sutton, 1988. ix–lxiv.

———. *Writings Ascribed to Richard Rolle: Hermit of Hampole*. New York: D.C. Heath, 1927.

Allen, Rosamund S. "Tactile and Kinesthetic Imagery in Richard Rolle's Works". *Mystics Quarterly* 13.1 (1987): 12–18.

Althaus-Reid, Marcella. *Indecent Theology: Theological Perversions in Sex, Gender, and Politics*. Routledge: New York, 2000.

———. *The Queer God*. London: Routledge, 2003.

Arons, Wendy and Theresa J. May. "Introduction." *Readings in Performance and Ecology*. Eds. Wendy Arons and Theresa J. May. New York: Palgrave MacMillan, 2012. 1–10.

Asad, Talal. *Genealogies of Religion: Discipline and Reasons of Power in Christianity and Islam*. Baltimore: The Johns Hopkins University Press, 1993.

Astell, Ann W. "Feminine *Figurae* in the Writings of Richard Rolle: A Register of Growth." *Mystics Quarterly* 15.3 (1989): 117–124.

———. *The Song of Songs in the Middle Ages*. Ithaca: Cornell University Press, 1990.

B

The Basic Writings of Aristotle. Ed. Richard McKeon. New York: Random House, 1941.

Belisle, Peter-Damian. *The Language of Silence: The Changing Face of Monastic Solitude*. Maryknoll: Orbis, 2003.

Bell, Nicholas. *Music in Medieval Manuscripts*. Toronto: University of Toronto Press, 2011.

St. Benedict, *The Rule of Saint Benedict*. Ed. Thomas Fry. New York: Vintage Spiritual Classics, 1981.

Biddle, Mark E. *Missing the Mark: Sin and Its Consequences in Biblical Theology*. Nashville: Abingdon, 2005.

Blesser, Barry and Linda-Ruth Salter, "Ancient Acoustic Spaces." *The Sound Studies Reader*. Ed. Jonathan Sterne. London: Routledge, 2012. 186–196.

Bloomfield, Morton. *The Seven Deadly Sins*. East Lansing: Michigan State University Press, 1967.

Boenig, Robert. "St. Augustine's *Jubilus* and Richard Rolle's *Canor*." *Vox Mystica: Essays on Medieval Mysticism in Honor of Professor Valerie M. Lagorio*. Eds. Anne Clark Bartlett, Thomas H. Bestul, Janet Goebel, and William F. Pollard. Cambridge: DS Brewer, 1995. 75–86.

Boffy, Julia. "Middle English Lyrics and Manuscripts." *A Companion to the Middle English Lyric*. Ed. Thomas G. Duncan. Cambridge: D.S. Brewer, 2005. 1–18.

Bonde, Sheila and Clark Mannes. "Performing Silence and Regulating Sound: the Monastic Soundscape of Saint-Jean-Des-Vignes." *Resounding Images: Medieval Intersections of Art, Music, and Sound*. Eds. Susan Boynton and Diane J. Reilly. Turnhout: Brepols, 2015. 47–70.

The Book of Margery Kempe. Ed. Lynn Staley. Kalamazoo: TEAMS, 1996.

Bower, Calvin Martin. *Boethius' The Principles of Music: An Introduction, Translation, and Commentary*. Dissertation, George Peabody College for Teachers, 1967.

Brantley, Jessica. *Reading in the Wilderness*. Chicago: University of Chicago Press, 2007.

Burger, Glenn and Steven F. Kruger, "Introduction." *Queering the Middle Ages.* Eds. Glenn Burger and Steven F. Kruger. Minneapolis: University of Minnesota Press, 2001. xi-xxiv.

Burgwinkle, Bill. "Medieval Somatics." *The Cambridge Companion to the Body in Literature.* Eds. David Hillman and Ulrika Maude. Cambridge: Cambridge University Press, 2015. 10–23.

———. "Queer Theory and the Middle Ages." *French Studies* LX.I (2006): 79–88.

Burrus, Virginia. "Queer Father: Gregory of Nyssa and the Subversion of Identity." *Queer Theology: Rethinking the Western Body.* Ed. Gerard Loughlin. Malden, MA: Blackwell, 2007. 147–162.

———. *The Sex Lives of Saints: An Erotics of Ancient Hagiography.* Philadelphia: University of Pennsylvania Press, 2004.

Butterfield, Ardis. *The Familiar Enemy: Chaucer, Language, and Nation in the Hundred Years War.* Oxford: Oxford University Press, 2009.

Butler, Judith. *Gender Trouble: Feminism and the Subversion of Identity.* New York: Routledge, 1990.

———. *Giving an Account of Oneself.* New York: Fordham University Press, 2005.

C

The Cambridge Companion to Medieval English Mysticism. Eds. Samuel Fanous and Vincent Gillepsie. Cambridge: Cambridge University Press, 2011.

Caputo, John. *The Insistence of God: A Theology of Perhaps.* Bloomington: Indiana University Press, 2013.

———. *The Mystical Element in Heidegger's Thought.* New York: Fordham, 1986.

———. "On Not Knowing Who We Are: Madness, Hermeneutics, and the Night of Truth in Foucault." *Foucault and the Critique of Institutions.* Eds. John Caputo and Mark Yount. University Park, PA: Penn State University Press, 1993. 233–262.

———. *The Weakness of God: A Theology of the Event.* Bloomington: Indiana University Press, 2006.

Carette, Jeremy. "Rupture and Transformation: Foucault's Concept of Spirituality Reconsidered." *Foucault Studies* 15 (2013): 52–71.

Castelli, Elizabeth A. "History's Queer Touch: A Forum on Carolyn Dinshaw's *Getting Medieval: Sexualities and Communities, Pre- and Postmodern.*" *Journal of the History of Sexuality* 10 (2001): 165–166.

Cheng, Patrick S. *From Sin to Amazing Grace: Discovering the Queer Christ.* New York: Seabury, 2012.

———. *Radical Love.* New York: Seabury Books, 2011.

Chisolm, Dianne. "Biophilia, Creative Involution, and the Ecological Future of Queer Desire." *Queer Ecologies: Sex, Nature, Politics, and Desire.* Eds. Catriona

Mortimer-Sandilands and Bruce Erickson. Bloomington: Indiana University Press, 2010. 359–381.

Clark, J.P.H. "Richard Rolle as a Biblical Commentator." *Downside Review* 104.356 (1986): 165–213.

———. "Richard Rolle: A Theological Re-assessment." *The Downside Review* 101.343 (1983): 108–139.

Clay, Rotha Mary. *The Hermits and Anchorites of England.* London: Methuen, 1914.

The Cloud of Unknowing, Ed. Patrick J. Gallacher. Kalamazoo: TEAMS, 1997.

Coates, Peter A. "The Strange Stillness of the Past: Towards an Environmental History of Sound and Noise." *Sound Studies: Critical Concepts in Media and Cultural Studies*, Vol. I. Ed. Michael Bull. London: Routledge, 2013. 636–665.

Comper, Frances M.M. *The Life and Lyrics of Richard Rolle.* New York: Barnes and Noble, 1928.

Connolly, William. *The Fragility of Things: Self-Organizing Processes, Neoliberal Fantasies, and Democratic Activism.* Durham: Duke University Press, 2013.

———. *A World of Becoming.* Durham: Duke University Press, 2011.

Cornwall, Susannah. *Controversies in Queer Theology.* London: SCM Press, 2011.

Crane, Susan. *Animal Encounters: Contacts and Concepts in Medieval Britain.* Philadelphia: University of Pennsylvania Press, 2013.

Cunningham, Conor. *Genealogy of Nihilism: Philosophies of Nothing and the Difference of Theology.* New York: Routledge, 2002.

D

David, Carmel Bendon *Mysticism and Space: Spatiality in the Works of Richard Rolle, The Cloud of Unknowing Author, and Julian of Norwich.* Washington, D.C.: The Catholic University of America Press, 2008.

Davis, Virginia. "The Rule of Saint Paul the First Hermit." *Monks, Hermits, and the Ascetic Tradition.* Ed. W. J. Sheils. Padstow: T. J. Press, 1985. 203–214.

Diehl, Patrick S. *The Medieval European Religious Lyric: An Ars Poetica.* Berkeley: University of California Press, 1985.

Dinshaw, Carolyn. "Chaucer's Queer Touches/A Queer Touches Chaucer." *Exemplaria* 7.1 (1994): 75–92.

———. "Got Medieval?" *Journal of the History of Sexuality* 10 (2001): 202–212.

———. *Getting Medieval: Sexualities and Communities, Pre- and Post-modern.* Durham: Duke University Press, 1999.

———. *How Soon Is Now? Medieval Texts, Amateur Readers, and the Queerness of Time.* Durham: Duke University Press, 2012.

Doyle, A.I. "Carthusian Participation in the Movement of Works of Richard Rolle Between England and Other Parts of Europe in the 14th and 15th Centuries." *Kartäusermystik und–mystiker, Analecta Carthusiana* 55.2 (1981): 109–20.
Dronke, Peter. *The Medieval Lyric*. Cambridge: D.S. Brewer, 1996.
———. "The Song of Songs and Medieval Love-Lyric." *The Bible and Medieval Culture*. Eds. W. Lourdaux and D. Verhelst. Leuven: Leuven University Press, 1979. 236–62.
Duns Scotus, John. "Parisian Proof for the Existence of God." Eds. William A. Frank and Allan B. Wolter, *Duns Scotus Metaphysician*. West Lafayette, IN: Purdue University Press, 1995. 40–107.
Dyson, Michael Eric. *Pride*. Oxford: Oxford University Press, 2006.

E

Ehrenreich, Barbara. *Living with a Wild God*. New York: Twelve, 2014.
Edelman, Lee. *No Future: Queer Theory and the Death Drive*. Durham: Duke University Press, 2004.

F

"Fact Check: McCrory's "Myths vs Facts" email on HB2." http://www.wral.com/fact-check-mccrory-s-myths-vs-facts-email-on-hb2/15605025/.
Flynn, William T. "'The Soul is Symphonic': Meditation on Luke 15:25 and Hildegard of Bingen's Letter 23." *Music and Theology: Essays in Honor of* Robin A. *Leaver*. Ed. David Zager. Lanham, MD: The Scarecrow Press, 2007. 1–8.
Freccero, Carla. "Queer Times." *South Atlantic Quarterly* 106.3 (2007): 485–493.
Foucault, Michel. "28 March 1984: First Hour." *The Courage of Truth: The Government of Self and Others II, Lectures at the College de France 1983–1984*. Ed. Frédéric Gross. Trans. by Graham Burchell. New York: Palgrave MacMillian, 2011. 307–325.
———. "About the Beginning of the Hermeneutics of the Self." *Religion and Culture: Michel Foucault*. Ed. Jeremy Carette. New York: Routledge, 1999. 158–181.
———. *Discipline and Punish*. 2nd. Ed. Trans. Alan Sheridan. New York: Vintage Books, 1995.
———. *The History of Sexuality Volume One: An Introduction*. Trans. Robert Hurley. New York: Vintage, 1995.
———. *The History of Sexuality Volume Two: The Use of Pleasure*. Trans. Robert Hurley. New York: Vintage, 1985.
———. *The History of Sexuality Volume Three: The Care of the Self*. Trans. Robert Hurley. New York: Vintage, 1988.

———. *On the Government of the Living: Lectures at the College de France, 1979–1980.* Ed. Michael Senellart. New York: Palgrave MacMillan, 2012.
———. "Pastoral Power and Political Reason." *Religion and Culture: Michel Foucault.* Ed. Jeremy R. Carette. New York: Routledge, 1999. 135–153.
———. "A Preface to Transgression." *Religion and Culture: Michel Foucault.* Ed. Jeremy R. Carette. New York: Routledge, 1999. 57–71.
———. *Security, Territory, Population: Lectures at the College de France 1977–78*, Ed. Michel Senellart. Trans. Graham Burchell. New York: Palgrave, 2004.
———. "Sexuality and Power (1978)," *Religion and Culture: Michel Foucault.* Ed. Jeremy R. Carette. New York: Routledge, 1999. 115–130.
Freeman, Elizabeth. *Time Binds: Queer Temporalities, Queer Histories.* Durham: Duke University Press, 2010.

G

Galvez, Marisa. *Songbook: How Lyrics Became Poetry in Medieval Europe.* Chicago: University of Chicago Press, 2012.
General Assembly of North Carolina. Second Special Session 2016. Session Law 2016-3. House Bill 2. http://www.ncleg.net/Sessions/2015E2/Bills/House/PDF/H2v4.pdf.
Goldberg, Jonathan and Madhavi Menon. "Queering History." *PMLA* 120 (2005): 1608–1617.
Gray, Douglas. *Themes and Images in the Medieval English Religious Lyric.* London: Routledge, 1972.
Grimlaicus. *The Rule for Solitaries.* Trans. Andrew Thornton. Collegeville, MN: Liturgical Press, 2011.

H

Hale, Rosemary Drage. "'Taste and See for God is Sweet': Sensory Perception and Memory in Medieval Christian Mystical Experience," *Vox Mystica: Essays on Medieval Mysticism in Honor of* Valerie M. *Lagorio.* Ed. Anne Clarke Bartlett. Rochester: D.S. Brewer, 1995. 3–14.
Halperin, David M. *Saint Foucault: Towards a Gay Hagiography.* Oxford: Oxford University Press, 1995.
Hanna, Ralph. *The English Manuscripts of Richard Rolle: A Descriptive Catalogue.* Exeter: University of Exeter Press, 2010.
———. "The Middle English *Vitae Patrum* Collection." *Mediaeval Studies* 49 (1987): 411–435.
———. *Richard Rolle: Uncollected Prose and Verse.* Ed. Ralph Hanna. Oxford: Oxford University Press, 2007.
Harman, Graham. *Guerilla Metaphysics.* Chicago: Open Court, 2005.

———. *The Quadruple Object*. Winchester UK: Zero Books, 2011.
Hart, Kevin. "Absolute Interruption: On Faith." *Questioning God*. Eds. John D. Caputo, Mark Dooley, and Michael J. Scanlon. Blooming: Indiana University Press, 2001. 186–208.
Hassel, Julia. *Choosing Not to Marry: Women and Autonomy in the Katherine Group*. New York: Routledge, 2002.
Heidegger, Martin. *The Phenomenology of Religious Life*. Trans. Matthias Fritsch and Jennifer Anna Gosetti-Ferencei. Bloomington: Indiana University Press, 2010.
———. *Ontology—the Hermeneutics of Facticity*. Trans. John van Buren. Bloomington: Indiana University Press, 2008.
Hennessy, M.V. "The Remains of the Royal Dead in an English Carthusian Manuscript, London, British Library, MS Additional 37049." *Viator* 33 (2002): 310–354.
Herlinger, Jan "Music Theory of the Fourteenth and Early Fifteenth Centuries." *Music as Concept and Practice in the Late Middle Ages*. Eds. Reinhard Strohm and Bonnie J. Blackburn. Oxford: Oxford University Press, 2001. 244–300.
Hermitary: Resources and Reflections on Hermits and Solitude. http://www.hermitary.com/articles/benediction.html. (March 2016).
Higgs, Laquita. "Richard Rolle and His Concern for 'Even Christians'." *Mystics Quarterly* 14.4 (1988): 177–185.
Hillier, Paul. *A Performer's Guide to Medieval Music*. Ed. Ross W. Duffin. Bloomington: Indiana University Press, 2000.
Hilton, Walter. "The Mixed Life." *Richard Rolle and His Followers*. Ed. C. Horstmann. Cambridge: DS Brewer, 1999. 264–292.
Hollywood, Amy. "The Normal, the Queer, and the Middle Ages." *Journal of the History of Sexuality* 10 (2001): 173–179.
———. "Queering the Beguins: Mechtild of Magdeburg, Hadewijch of Anvers, Marguerite Porete." *Queer Theology: Rethinking the Western Body*. Ed. Gerard Loughlin. Malden, MA: Blackwell, 2007. 163–175.
Holsinger, Bruce W. *Music, Body, and Desire in Medieval Culture: Hildegard of Bingen to Chaucer*. Stanford: Stanford University Press, 2001.
Honnefelder, Ludger. "The Concept of Nature in Medieval Metaphysics." *Nature in Medieval Thought: Some Approaches East and West*. Ed. Chumaru Koyama. Leiden: Brill, 2000. 75–93.
Hoogland, Cornelia. "Sound Ecology in the Woods: Red Riding Hood Takes an Audio Walk." *Readings in Performance and Ecology*. Eds. Wendy Arons and Theresa J. May. New York: Palgrave MacMillan, 2012. 181–190.
Hsy, Jonathan. *Trading Tongues: Merchants, Multilingualism, and Medieval Literature* Columbus: Ohio State University Press, 2013.
Hudson, Anne. *Two Revisions of Rolle's English Psalter Commentary and the Related Canticles*. EETS. no. 340. Oxford: Oxford University Press, 2012.

Hughes, Jonathan. *Pastors and Visionaries: Religion and Secular Life in Late Medieval Yorkshire.* Woodbridge: Boydell, 1988.

I

An Illustrated Yorkshire Carthusian Religious Miscellany British Library London Additional MS. 37049. Ed. James Hogg. Salzburg: Institut Fur Anglistik Und Amerikanistik, 1981.

Ingold, Tim. *Being Alive: Essays in Movement, Knowledge, and Description.* London: Routledge, 2011.

J

Jagose, Annemarie. *Queer Theory: An Introduction.* New York: New York University Press, 1997.

Jantzen, Grace. "Contours of a Queer Theology" *Feminism and Theology.* Eds. Janet Martin Soskice and Diana Lipton. Oxford: Oxford University Press, 2003. 276–285.

———. *Power, Gender, Mysticism.* Cambridge: Cambridge UP, 1995.

Jennings, Margaret. "Richard Rolle and the Three Degrees of Love." *The Downside Review* 93 (1975): 193–200.

Jennings, Jr., Theodore W. *The Man Jesus Loved: Homoerotic Narratives from the New Testament.* Cleveland: Pilgrim, 2003.

Jenkins, Willis. *Ecologies of Grace: Environmental Ethics and Christian Theology.* Oxford: Oxford University Press, 2008.

Johnson, Eleanor. *Practicing Literary Theory in the Middle Ages.* Chicago: University of Chicago Press, 2013.

K

Kane, Brian. *Sound Unseen: Acousmatic Sound in Theory and Practice.* Oxford: Oxford University Press, 2014.

Kaufmann, Stuart A. *Reinventing the Sacred: A New View of Science, Reason, and Religion.* New York: Basic Books, 2008.

King, Peter. "Scotus on Metaphysics." *The Cambridge Companion to Duns Scotus.* Ed. Thomas Williams. Cambridge: Cambridge University Press, 2003. 15–69.

Knowlton, Mary Arthur. *The Influence of Richard Rolle and of Julian of Norwich on the Middle English Lyrics.* Paris: Mouton, 1973.

Kruger, Steven F. "Medieval/Postmodern: HIV/AIDS and the Temporality of Crisis." *Queering the Middle Ages,* Eds. Glenn Burger and Steven F. Kruger. Minneapolis: University of Minnesota Press, 2001. 252–283.

Kuczynski, Michael P. *Prophetic Songs: The Psalms as Moral Discourse in Late Medieval England.* Philadelphia: University of Pennsylvania Press, 1995.
———. "The Psalms and Social Action in Late Medieval England." *The Place of the Psalms in the Intellectual Culture of the Middle Ages.* Ed. Nancy Van Deusen. Albany: State University of New York Press, 1999. 199–214.

L

Labat, Èlisabeth-Paule. *The Song That I Am: On the Mystery of Music.* Trans. Erik Varden. Collegeville, MN: Cistercian Publications, 2014.
Larrimore, Mark. "Introduction." *Queer Christianities: Lived Religion in Transgressive Forms.* Eds. Kathleen T. Talvacchia, Michael F. Pettinger, and Mark Larrimore. New York: New York University Press, 2015. 1–10.
Lawlor, Leonard. *Derrida and Husserl: The Basic Problem of Phenomenology.* Bloomington: Indiana University Press, 2002.
Leyser, Henrietta. *Hermits and the New Monasticism: A Study of Religious Communities in Western Europe 1000–1150.* London: MacMillan Press, 1984.
License, Tom. *Hermits and Recluses in English Society: 950–1200.* Oxford: Oxford University Press, 2011.
Lochrie, Kamra. "The Language of Transgression: Body, Flesh, and Word in Mystical Discourse." *Speaking Two Languages: Traditional Disciplines and Contemporary Theory in Medieval Studies.* Ed. Allen J. Frantzen. New York: State University of New York Press, 1991. 115–140.
———. "Mystical Acts, Queer Tendencies." *Constructing Medieval Sexuality.* Eds. Karma Lochrie, Peggy McCracken, and James A. Schultz. Minneapolis: University of Minnesota Press, 1997. 180–200.
Luxford, Julian M. "Precept and Practice: The Decorations of English Carthusian Books." *Studies in Carthusian Monasticism in the Late Middle Ages.* Ed. Julian Luxford. Brepols: Turnout, 2009. 225–267.

M

Machan, Tim William. *The Ecology of Middle English.* Oxford: Oxford University Press, 2003.
Marion, Jean-Luc. *God Without Being.* Trans. Thomas A Carlson. Chicago: University of Chicago Press, 1991.
Markus, R.A. "De Civitate Die: Pride and the Common Good." *Proceedings of the PMR Conference* 12–13 (1987): 1–16.
McDaniel, Rhonda. "Pride Goes Before a Fall: Aldhelm's Practical Application of Gregorian and Cassianic Conceptions of *Superbia* and the Eight Principal

Vices." *The Seven Deadly Sins: From Communities to Individuals.* Ed. Richard Newhauser. Leiden: Brill, 2007. 95–109.

Matter, E. Ann. *The Voice of My Beloved: The Song of Songs in Western Medieval Christianity.* Philadelphia: University of Pennsylvania Press, 1990.

McNamer, Sarah. *Affective Meditation and the Invention of Medieval Compassion.* Philadelphia: University of Pennsylvania Press, 2010.

McSweeney, John P. "Religion in the Web of Immanence: Foucault and Thinking Otherwise after the Death of God." *Foucault Studies* 15 (Feb 2013): 72–94.

Mills, Robert. *Seeing Sodomy in the Middle Ages.* Chicago: University of Chicago Press, 2015.

———. "'Whatever you do is a deligh to me!' Masculinity, Masochism, and Queer Play in Representations of Male Martyrdom." *Exemplaria* 13.1 (2001): 1–37.

Adam S. Miller, *Speculative Grace: Bruno Latour and Object Oriented Theology.* New York: Fordham, 2013.

McIlroy, Claire Elizabeth. *English Prose Treatises of Richard Rolle.* Cambridge: D.S. Brewer, 2004.

Morton, Timothy. *The Ecological Thought.* Cambridge: Harvard University Press, 2010.

Moyes, Malcolm Robert. *Richard Rolle's Expositio Super Novem Lectiones Mortuorum, Volume I.* Salzburg: Institut für Anglistik und Amerikanistik, 1988.

Muñoz, José Esteban. *Cruising Utopia.* New York: New York University Press, 2009.

N

Nancy, Jean-Luc. *Being Singular Plural.* Trans. Robert D. Richardson and Anne E. O'Byrne. Stanford: Stanford University of Press: 2000.

——— "The Deconstruction of Christianity." *Religion and Media.* Trans. Simon Sparks. Eds. Hent de Vries and Samuel Weber. Stanford: Stanford University Press, 2001. 115–130.

——— *Disenclosure: The Deconstruction of Christianity.* New York: Fordham University Press, 2008.

Nelstrop, Louise. "The Merging of Eremitic and "Affectivist" Spirituality in Richard Rolle's Reshaping of Contemplation." *Viator: A Journal of Medieval and Renaissance Studies* 35 (2004): 289–309.

Neugebauer, Cimaron. "Singer of punk rock band Against Me! burns birth certificate in protest of HB2." http://kutv.com/news/entertainment/singer-of-punk-rock-band-against-me-burns-birth-certificate-in-protest-of-hb2.

Nicholas, Lucy. *Queer Post-Gender Ethics: The Shape of Selves to Come.* New York: Palgrave MacMillan, 2014.

O

The Officium and Miracula of Richard Rolle, of Hampole. Ed. Reginald Maxwell Woolley. New York: Macmillan, 1919.
Origen, "Commentary on John, Book I." *Origen.* Ed. Joseph W. Trigg. London, Routledge, 1998. 103–149.

P

Pike, Alfred. *A Theology of Music.* Toledo, OH: Gregorian Institute of America, 1953.
Pinch, Trevor and Karin Bijsterveld. "New Keys to the World of Sound." *The Oxford Handbook of Sound Studies.* Eds. Trevor Pinch and Karin Bijsterveld. Oxford: Oxford University Press, 2011. 1–41.
Pollard, William. "Richard Rolle and the 'Eye of the Heart'." *Mysticism and Spirituality in Medieval England*, Eds. William F. Pollard and Robert Boenig. Cambridge: D.S. Brewer, 1997. 85–105.
——— "The 'Tone of Heaven': Bonaventuran Melody and the Easter Psalm in Richard Rolle." *The Popular Literature of Medieval England.* Ed. Thomas J. Heffernan Knoxville: University of Tennessee Press, 1988. 252–276.
Pugh, Tison. *Chaucer's (Anti-)eroticisms and the Queer Middle Ages.* Columbus: Ohio State University Press, 2014.
——— *Queering Medieval Genres.* New York: Palgrave MacMillan, 2004.

Q

Queer Christianities: Lived Religion in Transgressive Forms. Eds. Kathleen T. Talvacchia, Michael F. Pettinger, and Mark Larrimore. New York: New York University Press, 2015.

R

Religion and Sexism: Images of Women in the Jewish and Christian Traditions, Ed. Rosemary Radford Reuther. Eugene, OR: Wipf and Stock, 1988.
Relihan, Jr., Robert. "Richard Rolle and the Tradition of Thirteenth Century Devotional Literature." *Fourteenth Century English Mystics Newsletter* 4.4. (1978): 10–16.
Richard of St. Victor. *Benjamin Minor.* Trans. Anne Chamberlain Garrison. Dissertation, Michigan State University, 1957.
Renevey, Denis. "Encoding and Decoding: Metaphorical Discourse of Love in Richard Rolle's Commentary on the First Verses of the Song of Songs."

The Medieval Translator 4. Eds. Roger Ellis and Ruth Evans. Binghamton: Medieval and Renaissance Texts and Studies, 1994. 200–17.

———. *Language of Self and Love: Hermeneutics in the Writings of Richard Rolle and the Commentaries on the Song of Songs*. Cardiff: University of Wales Press, 2001.

Rolle, Richard. *Desyr and Delit. Richard Rolle: Prose and Verse*. Ed. S.J. Ogilvie-Thomson. EETS. no. 293. Oxford: Oxford University Press, 1988. 40–41.

———. "*Diliges Dominum* (Dublin Version)." *Richard Rolle: Uncollected Prose and Verse*. Ed. Ralph Hanna. EETS. no. 329. Oxford: Oxford University Press, 2007. 58–83.

———. "*Ego Dormio.*" *Richard Rolle: Prose and Verse*. Ed. S.J. Ogilvie-Thomson. EETS. no. 293. Oxford: Oxford University Press, 1988. 26–33.

———. *The English Writings*. Ed. Rosamund Allen. New York: Paulist Press, 1988.

———. *The Fire of Love*. Ed. and Trans. Clifton Wolters. London: Penguin, 1972.

———. *The Form of Living. Richard Rolle: Prose and Verse*. EETS. no. 293. Ed. S.J. Ogilvie-Thomson. Oxford: Oxford University Press, 1988. 1–25.

———. *Incendium Amoris*. Ed. Margaret Deanesly. New York: Longman, 1915.

———. "Lyrics." *English Writings of Richard Rolle, Hermit of Hampole*. Ed. Hope Emily Allen. Gloucester: Alan Sutton, 1988. 37–53.

———. *The Melos Amoris of Richard Rolle of Hampole*. Ed. E.J.F. Arnould. Oxford: Basil Blackwell, 1957.

———. *The Psalter or Psalms of David and Certain Canticles*, Ed. H.R. Bramley. Oxford: Clarendon Press, 1884.

Roper, Gregory. "The Middle English Lyric 'I,' Penitential Poetics, and Medieval Selfhood." *Poetica* 42 (1994): 71–103.

Rose, Nikolas. *Governing the Soul: The Shaping of the Private Self.* 2nd. Ed. London: Fress Association, 1999.

Rosenthal, Constance L. The *Vitae Patrum* in Old and Middle English Literature. Dissertation, U Penn, Philadelphia, 1936.

Ross, Alex. "Forward." *The Place Where You Go to Listen: In Search of an Ecology of Music*.Ed.John Luther Adams. Middletown, CT: Wesleyan University Press, 2009.

Rudy, Gordon. *Mystical Language of Sensation in the Middle Ages*. New York: Routledge, 2002.

S

Sauer, Michelle M. "Uncovering Difference: Encoded Homoerotic Anxiety within the Christian Eremitic Tradition in Medieval England." *Journal of the History of Sexuality* 19.1 (2010): 133–152.

Scotus, John Duns. "Concerning Human Knowledge." *Philosophical Writings*. Ed. and Trans. Allan Wolter. Indianapolis: Hackett, 1987. 96–132.

Sedgwick, Eve Kosowsky. *Between Men: English Literature and Male Homosocial Desire.* New York: Columbia University Press, 1985.
———. *Epistemology of the Closet.* Berkeley: University of California Press, 1990.
The Sexual Theologian: Essays on Sex, God, and Politics. Eds. Marcella Althaus-Reid and Lisa Isherwood. London: T&T Clark, 2004.
Stuart, Elizabeth. "Sacremental Flesh." *Queer Theology: Rethinking the Christian Body.* Ed. Gerard Loughlin. Malden, MA: Blackwell, 2007. 65–75.

T

Tanner, Norman. *Ages of Faith: Popular Religion in Late Medieval England and Western Europe.* London: I.B. Tauris, 2009.
Tonstad, Linne Marie. *God and Difference: The Trinity, Sexuality, and the Transformation of Finitude.* New York: Routledge, 2016.
Two Revisions of Rolle's English Psalter Commmentary and the Related Canticles. Ed. Anne Hudson. Oxford: EETS, 2012.

V

Vauchez, André. *Francis of Assisi: The Life and Afterlife of a Medieval Saint.* Trans. Michael F. Cusato. New Haven: Yale University Press, 2012.

W

Wakelin, M.F. "Richard Rolle and the Language of Mystical Experience in the Fourteenth Century." *Downside Review* 97 (1979): 192–203.
Ward, Graham. "Questioning God." *Questioning God.* Eds. John D. Caputo, Mark Dooley, and Michael J. Scanlon. Bloomington: Indiana University Press, 2001. 274–290.
Warner, Michael. "Tongues Untied: Memoirs of a Pentecostal Boyhood." *The Material Queer: A LesBiGay Cultural Studies Reader.* Ed. Donald Morton. Boulder, CO: Westview Press, 1996. 215–224.
Warren, Nancy. *Anchorites and Their Patrons in Medieval England.* Berkley: University of California Press, 1985.
Watson, Nicholas. *Richard Rolle and the Invention of Authority.* Cambridge: Cambridge University Press, 1991.
Weiss, Gail. "The Body as a Narrative Horizon." *Thinking the Limits of the Body.* Eds. Jeffrey Jerome Cohen and Gail Weiss. Albany: State University of New York Press, 2003. 25–38.
Wenzel, Siegfried. "The Seven Deadly Sins: Some Problems of Research." *Speculum* 43 (1968): 1–22.

Whitehead, Alfred North. *Process and Reality*. New York: The Free Press, 1978.
———. *Religion in the Making*. Cambridge: Cambridge University Press, 2011.
Whitehead, Christiana. "Middle English Religious Lyrics." *A Companion to the Middle English Lyric*. Ed. Thomas G. Duncan. Cambridge: D.S. Brewer, 2005. 96–11.
Wilcox, Annabelle. "Phenomenology, Embodiment, and Political Efficacy." *The Ashgate Research Companion to Queer Theory*. Eds. Noreen Giffney and Michael O'Rourke. Burlington, VT: Ashgate, 2010. 95–110.
Wilsbacher, Greg. J. "Something Queer is Going ON: Sex and Methodology in the Middle Ages." *College Literature* 30.2 (2003): 195–203.
Woolf, Rosemary. *The English Religious Lyric in the Middle Ages*. Oxford: Clarendon, 1968.

Z

Zimmerman, Elizabeth. "'It is Not the Deed but the Intention of the Doer': The Ethic of Intention and Consent in the First Two Letters of Heloise." *Modern Language Studies* 42.3 (2006): 249–267.
Žižek, Slavoj. *The Fragile Absolute*. London: Verso, 2000.
Zumthor, Paul. *Towards a Medieval Poetics*. Trans. Phillip Bennett. Minneapolis: U of Minnesota P, 1992.

INDEX

A
Abjection, 63
Abstinence, 31
Acousmatic, 11, 19, 86, 87
Adams, John Luther, 87, 89, 91
Against Me!, 122
Agamben, Giorgio, 9
Ahmed, Sarah, 59, 62, 74
Albin, Andrew, 89, 92, 95, 97
Allen, Hope Emily, 98, 99, 105, 117, 118, 122n1
Althaus-Reid, Marcella, 3–4, 5, 26
Anchorhold, 5
Anchorite, 4, 5, 7, 10, 67
Ancrene Wisse, 34
Angel, 31, 33, 43, 62, 87, 92
Aquinas, Thomas, 11, 95, 112n66
Aristotle, 12, 18, 76
Augustine, 11, 17, 28, 56, 66

B
Being, 2, 3, 8, 12, 15, 17–19, 26–27, 29–31, 33, 34, 38–43, 45, 47–49, 55, 56, 58, 59, 61, 62, 66–68, 71, 72, 76, 79n17, 81n39, 86, 89, 90, 92, 95, 96, 98, 101, 102, 121, 122
Bernard of Clairvaux, 37, 79n17

BL MS Add 31042, 97
BL MS Add 37049, 97, 106, 112n68
Body
  open, 19, 35, 55–77, 121, 122
  seated, 73, 74
  sonorous, 87
Boethius, 88–89
  De Musica, 88
The Book of Margery Kempe, 122n5, 122n7
Burger, Glenn, 3
Butler, Judith, 15, 18

C
Canor, 19, 37, 56, 72, 77, 85–107, 121
Caputo, John, 80n21, 81n52, 101, 104
Carthusian, 10, 97, 105, 114n121, 120
Cheng, Patrick, 11, 43, 50n16
Christ
  as creator, 104
  Crucifixion, 100, 102
  as Eucharist, 103
  as lover, 100, 103
  as maker, 9
  name of, 47, 77, 86, 101, 103, 104
  Passion, 103

Circumcision, 68–69, 77
  spiritual, 68–69, 77
Clay, Rotha Mary, 7
The Cloud of Unknowing, 10, 33, 34
Cognition
  abstract, 58
  intuitive, 58
Cold, 32, 66, 68, 77
Comper, Frances, 10, 37
Conduct, 4, 6–7, 18, 96
Connolly, William, 33, 90
Contemplative, 2, 12, 14, 15, 16, 17–18, 19, 27, 29, 30, 32, 33–49, 60, 62, 63, 65, 67, 68–70, 72–77, 91, 93, 95, 107
CUL MS Dd. 5.64, 97
Cunningham, Conor, 56, 58, 63, 68, 79n18, 82n54

D

Deception, 25, 27, 29–32, 35, 40, 48, 56, 66
Dinshaw, Carolyn, 78n9, 122n1
Direction, 33, 47, 61, 66, 71–77
  Godwards, 75
Dulcor, 19, 56, 69, 121
  delyte, 69
Dwelling, 34, 36, 37, 38, 62, 74

E

Ecodramaturgy, 96
Ecology
  divine, 11, 19, 77, 91, 95
  song, 95
  wilderness, 106
Ecstasy, 9, 57, 119, 121
  song, 71, 86
Ehrenreich, Barbara, 118–119
Enclosed, 7, 31, 73, 92, 95

England, 7
  medieval, 7
Eremitic, 2–19, 25–50, 55–58, 60, 66, 67, 72, 73, 76, 87, 107
  identity, 8, 10, 11, 13, 14, 16, 17, 18, 26, 56
Erotohistoriography, 6
Eternity, 15, 33, 42, 56, 71
Ethics, 12, 14, 15, 18, 57, 98
Exegesis
  Book of Job, 36
  Corinthians, 69
  Jeremiah, 66
  Psalms, 34
  Song of Songs, 110n37
Exile, 4, 8, 17
Exomologesis, 5, 14–19
Eye of the heart, 34, 35, 36, 43

F

Fervor, 19, 27, 37, 56, 118, 121
Finitude, 50n2
Fire, 15, 19, 27, 34, 35, 42, 43, 46–48, 56, 58, 60–64, 65–72, 74, 75, 77, 98, 118–119, 122
Foucault, Michel
  The Government of the Living, 51n20
  Security, Territory, Population, 21n25
Franciscans, 5
Freeman, Elizabeth, 6

G

Genre, 22n48, 46, 57, 86, 120
God
  Indwelling, 56, 65, 120
  Touch, 26, 29, 42, 49, 56, 57, 67–71, 72, 77, 86, 87
  Sound, 19, 86, 87, 90, 91
Grace, Laura Jane, 122

INDEX   141

Gregory the Great, 11
Grimlaicus, 4
Rule for Solitaries, 4

H
Hagiography, 41, 57, 119, 120, 121
Hanna, Ralph, 13, 113n76
Harman, Graham, 62, 64, 65
Harmonics, 86, 88, 89, 95, 121
  divine, 95
HB2, 122
Heart
  dwelling, 62
  fire, 34, 35, 43, 46, 47, 56, 62–67, 68, 70, 71, 72, 77, 121
Heidegger, Martin, 56, 61, 66, 67, 80n21, 81n39
Heretic, 16, 73
Hermit
  becoming, 18, 56, 73
  process, 18, 26, 27
  rule, 4, 8, 9
Hilton, Walter, 10
Holiness, 14, 48
  hypocrites, 67
Holy, 13, 14, 15, 17, 31, 32, 33, 36, 41, 66, 70, 73, 103
Humility, 10, 12, 13, 15, 16, 48, 60
Hymn, 94

I
Imagination, 37, 60
Indwelling, 19, 56, 65, 74, 76, 102, 120
Intelligence, 41
Intentionality, 11, 14–19, 59, 62, 77

J
Jagose, Annemarie, 2
Jantzen, Grace, 30

Julian of Norwich, 62, 118

K
Kempe, Margery, 118–119
Kenosis, 13
Kirkby, Margaret, 10, 29, 45, 67
Kotsko, Adam, 71, 72
Kruger, Steven F., 3

L
Langland, William, 7
Language
  mystical, 33, 56, 64
  sensory, 72
Lincoln Cathedral MS 91, 97
Listening
  exploratory, 91
  synthetic, 91
Liturgy, 114n102
Lochrie, Karma, 63, 91
Lollards and Lollardry, 73, 92, 110n42
Longleat MS 29, 97
Love
  colocality, 34, 45–46
  ethos, 43–50
  gift, 48
  heart, 48
  inseparabile, 45–46
  insuperabile, 45
  praxis, 27
  synguler, 45, 46
Lyric
  religious, 90
  wilderness, 106

M
Meditation, 29, 56, 60, 62, 73, 77, 89, 95, 102, 104, 106

Metaphor, 26, 33, 38, 49, 64, 65, 66, 67, 77, 92
Mills, Robert, 20n5
Monastery, 4, 6, 7
Monasticism, 5, 96
Monks, 5, 73, 115n124
Morton, Timothy, 95, 97, 114n114
Moyes, Malcolm, 59, 79n17
Munoz, José Esteban, 3
Musica speculativa, 88
Myrour of Recluses, 4

N

Nancy, Jean-Luc, 58, 83n73, 83n76
Narrative, 15, 26, 57, 58, 63, 119
Normativity, 12, 29

O

Object, 6, 26, 30, 40, 47, 48, 49, 57, 60, 62, 64, 65, 67, 69, 71, 74, 82n68, 86, 90, 95, 98, 102, 104
Object-oriented ontology (OOO), 64
Ontology, 2, 11, 18, 25–50, 55, 64, 65–66, 75, 86
Origen, 41

P

Parrhesia, 18
Pastoral power, 6, 7, 8, 9, 12
Pelagius, 11
Penance, 13, 17, 31, 32
Performance, 10, 43, 56, 57, 86, 90, 91, 96, 97, 107

Phenomenology, 2, 11, 18, 19, 26, 49, 55–77
Post-structuralism, 2, 3
Protrepsis, 57
Psalter, 92, 93, 95
Pugh, Tison, 2, 22n48, 91

Q

Queer
 capability, 36, 49, 50, 56, 67
 ecology, 2, 18, 26
 identity, 2, 3, 12, 18
 object, 26, 27, 57, 74
 ontology, 26
 phenomenology, 60, 62
 potential, 91
 pride, 4, 12, 14, 29
 song, 19, 56, 60, 61, 68, 76, 87, 91, 107
 space, 10, 32–38
 temporality, 19, 33, 37, 98, 101, 104
 theology, 3, 4, 9, 26, 29, 30, 59
 theory, 3, 19, 27
 time, 32–38, 41

R

Renevey, Denis, 109n32
Richard II, 8
Rolle, Richard
 Desyre and Delit, 60, 68
 Ego Dormio, 60, 69, 70, 71, 97, 106, 107
 English Psalter, 92, 110n42
 Epistle of St. Machari, 13
 Expositio Super Novem Lectiones, 59
 The Fire of Love, 35, 71, 75

The Form of Living, 27, 29, 30, 35, 43, 44, 45, 47, 49, 67
Incendium Amoris, 13, 43, 57, 60, 62, 65–67, 69, 77, 89, 97, 98, 120
Lyrics, 3, 19, 47, 86–88, 91, 92, 94–98, 101, 104–107; Gastly Gladnesse, 105; Salutation to Jesus, 103; A Song of the Love of Jesus, 98; A Song of the Love-Longing to Jesus, 102, 105
Melos Amoris, 108n19
Officium and *Miraculum*, 9, 10
Rose, Nikolas, 5, 13

S
Sacramental, 27
Saints, 4, 13, 96, 120
Scholasticism, 60, 79n17
Scotus, John Duns, 58, 67, 68
Scripture, 41
Sedgwick, Eve Kosowsky, 20n3, 20n4
Self
 external, 45–46
 inner, 36, 64
Senses
 hearing, 89, 118
 sight, 34–35
 taste, 13–14
 touch, 56, 60, 65, 118
Sight, 35–36, 86, 94
Sin
 lust, 4
 pride, 4, 11
 superbia, 11, 18
Sitting, 32, 37, 38, 49, 62, 71, 73, 74, 75–76
Solitary, 4, 7, 29–33, 35–38, 42
Solitude, 30, 32, 36, 37, 76

Somatics, 72
Song, 19, 37, 38, 42, 46, 47, 56, 58, 60, 61, 62, 65, 67, 68, 69, 71, 72, 74, 76–77, 85–89, 91–107, 118, 121
Soul, 8, 12, 16, 17, 19, 27, 29, 32–38, 42, 45, 46, 47, 49, 63, 69, 72, 75, 76, 77, 86, 92, 100, 102, 103
 dwelling, 36, 37, 38
Sound, 18–19, 86–103, 105–107
Soundscape, 86, 87–92, 96, 102, 107
Space
 material, 3
 spiritual, 74, 92
Speculative realism, 26
Stability
 mind, 75, 77
 sitting, 75
Sweetness, 18, 19, 36, 56, 58, 60, 61, 65, 67–71, 72, 73–74, 76, 77, 86, 119–121
 touch, 56, 67–71
Symphonia, 96, 101

T
Ten Commandments, 9, 40, 72, 93
Theology
 mystical, 3, 35, 61, 62
 queer, 3, 9, 26, 29, 30, 59
 systematic, 10
Thinghood, 27, 28, 32, 47
 thing-in-itself, 62
Thornton Dale, 9
Trinity, 27

U
Unknowing, 34, 36

V
Victorines, 79n17
  Richard of St. Victor, 66

W
Ward, Graham, 27–28
Watson, Nicholas, 10, 13, 35
Wilderness, 5, 36, 37, 38

Wisdom, 49, 70

Y
Yorkshire, 9, 20n14, 119

Z
Žižek, Slavoj, 28, 40

Printed in the United States
By Bookmasters